Development

for

Health

Selected articles from *Development in Practice*

Introduced by Eleanor Hill

A Development in Practice Reader

Series Editor: Deborah Eade

Oxfam (UK and Ireland)

Published by Oxfam (UK and Ireland)
First published 1997   .

Available from the following agents:
for Canada and the USA: Humanities Press International, 165 First Avenue,
Atlantic Highlands, New Jersey NJ 07716-1289, USA; tel. (908) 872 1441; fax (908)
872 0717
for southern Africa: David Philip Publishers, PO Box 23408, Claremont, Cape
Town 7735, South Africa; tel. (021) 644136; fax (021) 643358.

Available in Ireland from Oxfam in Ireland, 19 Clanwilliam Terrace, Dublin 2
(tel. 01 661 8544)

The views expressed in this book are those of the individual contributors, and not
necessarily those of the editors, the editorial advisers, or the publisher.

Published by Oxfam (UK and Ireland), 274 Banbury Road, Oxford OX2 7DZ, UK
(registered as a charity, no. 202918)

Designed by Oxfam Design Department
Typeset in Gill and Trump Mediaeval
Printed by Oxfam Print Unit
OX527/RB/97

Oxfam (UK and Ireland) is a member of Oxfam International.

Contents

Preface

Deborah Eade

Health and well-being are deeply personal matters. Nothing is more intimate than the experience of conceiving and bearing a child, and giving birth to a unique human being; none of us can live another's fear or pain; and death itself is something we cannot share, however real the grief we suffer. And yet it is precisely when we or those close to us face illness or chronic suffering that we perceive that health is in reality a very public issue. Policies which dictate what level of health-care provision is guaranteed, what kinds of service will be offered, how priorities are established between competing claims, where resources are concentrated, and what alternatives are available all become far more immediate when they affect us or our loved ones. Facing a particular health-related condition, and then being on the receiving end of the decisions or prejudices of others — be they health professionals, religious authorities, family members, neighbours, employers, or insurance companies — is something that often gives us a new awareness of how limited is our capacity to control some of the most central aspects of our lives. It gives us an insight into what exclusion feels like.

Disempowerment and exclusion are caused by a similar combination of personal experience and circumstances on the one hand and the social and political context on the other. The essays collected here show some of the complex ways and levels on which such exclusion operates, especially when people are already dealing with poverty, and what this means for their health status. At one end of the spectrum, we see the importance of the macro-economic and ideological settings. Economic policies that result in the under-funding of public services and the fragmentation of the regulatory role of government tend to reduce the threshold of what is considered an acceptable minimum standard of health-care provision for the population at large. Access to health care becomes dependent on the individual's capacity to pay: patients are turned from *citizens* who have rights and responsibilities into *clients* or *consumers* who can (if they can afford it, and if anyone will insure them) take their custom elsewhere. The question of financing health care may thus be posed as a pseudo-technical one: what kinds of cost-recovery and insurance mechanism 'work', and in what circumstances? The goal of 'Health for All by the Year 2000' is eroded into one of 'health for those who can pay today'.

In seeking to harmonise market forces with people's health and well-being, we risk overlooking the underlying question of whether health can or should be treated as a commodity. The figures are grim. During the 1980s, the number of people living in absolute poverty rose to over one billion, with the gap in *per capita* income between the industrial and developing worlds growing threefold between 1960 and 1993.

Each year, over 12 million children die of preventable causes before they reach adolescence. Average life expectancy in the richest countries is expected to rise to 79 years by the turn of the century; while it is expected actually to fall to 42 years in some of the poorest.[1] It is a commonplace to say that poverty and ill health are mutually reinforcing. And yet current trends suggest that 'the enjoyment of the highest attainable standard of health' which WHO describes as 'one of the fundamental rights of every human being' is seen almost as a by-product, something that will trickle down to the bottom some time in the future. There is a long way to trickle before this fundamental right reaches those who are destitute (currently one fifth of the human race), those who survive precariously in the informal sector, or those whose access to health care is limited by their age or their disabilities, or by armed conflict. And while seven out of ten of the world's poorest people are female, women's health needs are widely neglected, whatever their background. Yet, if development is not for health, what *is* it for — and who can expect to enjoy it?

Several essays in this compilation from *Development in Practice* examine the issue of exclusion from this angle. What are the forces that prevent women and men from taking advantage of the health services that are, theoretically, there for their benefit? Often the answers lie in the inappropriate ways in which such services are offered: expecting results too soon, ignoring other forms of knowledge and belief systems, imposing an agenda from above or outside, or failing to understand the complex social and power relations that affect people's behaviour and their expectations. A woman may have a right to ante-natal care, but if she does not know about it or why it matters, or if she cannot attend (whether because clinics are held at inconvenient times or inaccessible places, or because other family members do not allow her to go), then she may show up as a 'failure' in the midwife's performance. Exploring the many subtle ways in which disempowerment disables individuals and communities, the authors of the essays gathered here share their own practical experience of enabling people to develop the skills and the confidence to survive adversity, and to shape development in ways that better address their health-related needs.

The papers in this volume illustrate the issues addressed by Eleanor Hill in her introductory overview: how and why it is that people or aspects of health care are pushed to (or left in) the margins. They illustrate also her contention that it is often at these margins that ground-breaking (though unspectacular) achievements are made. Building on the insights of those who do not have power and status, and who lack many of the means to nurture their own health, reveals far more than the statistics can tell us about what is needed to ensure that development is for health — and about the consequences for humanity in failing to meet this challenge.

Deborah Eade
Editor, *Development in Practice*

Notes

1 Figures taken from *The World Health Report 1995: Bridging the Gap* (Geneva: WHO); and *Human Development Report 1996* (Oxford and New York: UNDP).

Over the edge:
health-care provision, development, and marginalisation

Eleanor Hill

'Health' is a broad subject. It involves anything from high-technology heart surgery to the simplest of home remedies for the common cold. The conditions and people dealt with by health practitioners also cover an enormous range: from compound fractures to schizophrenia; from infectious disease to alcoholism; from sufferers of arthritis to sufferers of torture. The context within which health care is provided varies across a number of dimensions: from centralised, government-controlled provision of a service which must cover an entire nation to small-scale private-sector provision either for profit or on a charitable basis, with all gradations in between; from professionally trained practitioners to provision of care in the home by family members. This is without the common distinctions of curative and preventative care, of public or community health and personal clinical requirements.

Health at the margins

The challenge is to find a way of addressing the topic from a clear perspective without losing sight of the need to deal with its complexity. The more I thought about the nature of *Development in Practice* as a journal and the working context of its readers, the more it seemed appropriate to focus on health and health-care provision at the margins. Even this leaves me with a broad

canvas to cover, as the nature of these margins differs from one context to another, but it is at the margins that needs are most likely to be most acute, as well as most often overlooked. It is also at the margins that we often find the most interesting and exciting work, the most challenging views. And it is by moving out to the margins that we can look back at the whole field and see what remains to be dealt with which is currently neglected.[1]

An example of the way in which a marginal situation can be liberating was shared with me by a colleague who worked in Angola throughout the civil war. He had been responsible for a hospital and a number of satellite facilities. The central hospital directed and controlled work for the entire programme, with little devolution of authority to staff at the periphery. As the war progressed, infrastructure deteriorated and travel between facilities became increasingly dangerous; gradually the old system became untenable. In order to keep facilities operational, it was necessary to allow them individual control of their programmes, priorities, and activities. Despite the persistent problems of working in a context of armed conflict, this decentralisation allowed staff to continue to provide a health service, with positive effects on their morale.

Within this example it is easy to see how the definitions of what is central and what is marginal can alter very quickly as a situation evolves. Peripheral staff and facilities who were of little relevance in decision-making or policy-development become central figures as the locus of control alters. At the same time, the central facility of the hospital and its management become somewhat marginal to the everyday operation of the system as a whole. Within the new context, other margins would become evident and claim attention. This changing nature of the margins in relation to health and health-care provision means that it is essential to keep analysing and reviewing any situation. Focusing on the margins helps us to avoid complacency through this constant requirement for re-analysis.

Where do the margins lie?

How to define the margins? One of the simplest means is to begin with those areas where health is poorest and explore the way in which the situation of the people may be considered marginal. The first characteristic to spring to mind is that very often they are at the margins of prosperity, surviving with a minimum of resources. Physical marginalisation is another common feature. People may be many miles or hours distant from the centres of provision, prevented from reaching them by rough terrain or poor transportation systems. In addition they are often distant or marginal in a cultural and political sense, not belonging to the groups who hold power, speaking a minority language, or simply accorded no importance within the political decision-making process.

This pattern of marginalisation persists at both macro and micro levels, creating overlapping layers of exclusion. It is of course easy to generalise, to designate particular groups as marginalised and then focus attention on them as the most needy. An instant list is easy to construct: women, children, the elderly, the mentally and physically disabled, the displaced. But it is vital also to consider the ways in which people overcome or overturn such situations, how they manage despite all expectations to maintain some control and a central position in aspects of

their lives. In short, we must enter into the real complexity of each situation to discover where its margins are and who operates at these margins. It is this which presents the most exciting and most difficult challenge, as it constantly confronts us with the assumptions we make and the stereotypes we construct, demanding that we reconsider over and over again how we make sense of the world.

Another anecdote may help to illustrate this. I remember watching a TV documentary about the Maasai in East Africa, featuring a ritual through which women could overcome infertility. As the programme went on, it appeared to me that these women, for whom infertility is an extreme misfortune, were entirely without power and destined to remain at the margins of their community. Without children as proof of their value to the community, they were of little consequence, and even this small chance of altering their plight was to be denied them. But just as I was reaching a point of equal sadness and anger on their behalf, the position changed. An older woman counselled the younger ones who needed the ritual to threaten the men with tears if they did not oblige in preparing for the ceremony. To an outsider this seemed an idle threat, of no particular consequence: women's tears are a frequent enough occurrence, but they do not often seem to bring dramatic change. In this context, however, the threat of them was sufficient. Power can be exercised in many ways, some of them unexpected and unrealised, and it is this which defines who counts as central and who counts as marginal within any specific setting.

The margins within the health service

It is not only the general population who can be marginalised in this way. The same is often true of those who are charged with providing them with health care. Practitioners too may be struggling to operate with few resources, in a context where the bulk of a budget is spent on maintaining central facilities. They may be isolated from professional discourse and discussion, from the latest ideas and technology. In fact they often suffer a double marginalisation, for in addition to this professional isolation, they may well be isolated from the population around them. This separation has educational, cultural, and psychosocial dimensions, as all these factors operate to create distance between the professionally trained health practitioner and the lay population. This distance may be expected by those such as myself when choosing to work in a completely different culture, but it is just as acute when one is working within one's own culture. I have been forcibly struck in the past by how little I knew of the realities of living on State benefit, or of surviving in a violent domestic situation; yet these are the realities for many of the women I met as a working midwife.

In a very real sense a health service can be viewed in the same way as any other community with similar distribution patterns of power and control. It can be hard for those working on the periphery to believe in their own capacity to take decisions or alter policy. Large bureaucratic institutions such as ministries of health do not lend themselves to flexible working practices. In many cases the training of health workers discourages them from showing too much initiative. Safety lies in following the prescribed procedures, carrying out tasks exactly as specified, and filling out the required reports to show that this is being done. This is perhaps especially true of non-medical staff, upon whom much of the burden of caring falls in developing countries. Yet it can be these same staff who are expected to encourage the community to become active and participate in decisions regarding health-care provision.

The following illustration is not unusual. For a range of reasons (international pressure, budgetary constraints, political insecurity), policy-makers decide that increased community participation is required to improve the efficiency of the health service,

especially in the remote rural areas where provision has always been problematic. They issue orders that committees must be formed, action plans drawn up, and local budgets prepared and submitted, all with the full participation of the local community. The local health worker is naturally a little apprehensive. Her initial training did not prepare her for this, and the few brief in-service sessions since she qualified are not enough to instil confidence. Besides which, she does not believe that the local community understands health issues properly. They never appear to take notice of her educational sessions, persisting in drawing water from the river. The communal latrines remain unused. How can she trust them to make decisions concerning health care? And who will get the blame if the monthly statistics show a deterioration in the health of the community? She will. The result is that she feels alienated from the community and abandoned and betrayed by the health service.

Counteracting this marginalisation within the health service is a difficult but crucial task, in which initial and on-going training are fundamental. Keeping curricula up to date in a rapidly changing world is not easy. Once trained, many health workers have no further contact with their training institutions and continue to work according to their original instruction. Others are desperate to advance their knowledge and skills, but face daunting barriers: funding is hard to acquire, study leave is rarely granted, family commitments can make it impossible for them to travel for studies.

Changing policy priorities

Another important way in which marginalisation occurs is through the changing priorities of health-care practitioners and policy-makers. The direction of the endeavour of health professionals can be deeply affected by the current fashions within these professions, not only by determining which specific conditions receive the attention of research teams, but also in terms of the approach followed in planning and delivering services. It is interesting to look back over the way this has differed through time and differing political contexts.

As with most aspects of human society, understanding of and attitudes towards health and illness have altered over time. Before the twentieth century, the commonest response to ill health was a pragmatic one of symptomatic care, rather than cure. Among much of the world's population this remains the predominant pattern. Certain well-known conditions may be deemed curable, but otherwise practitioners provide support and encouragement while the natural healing process occurs and (it is hoped) resolves the problem. Remedies have often been tested through generations, but may also have arisen through idiosyncratic individual belief. The priority among health practitioners is to provide emotional support and physical care, with an emphasis on the development of a good 'bedside manner' which will inspire confidence and so help healing. If death results, the humanity of the practitioner may be important in helping the bereaved to come to terms with their loss. Within this framework, the health worker is a rather marginal figure, of limited potency. The support obtained from family and social networks is a much more central consideration. Health, illness, and death are woven into the fabric of everyday life, and most individuals have a role to play in their maintenance or prevention. Ritual and ceremony are important in regulating the emotional burden which accompanies disease and death, placing those who perform these services in a prominent position.

More recently the allopathic medical approach became prevalent. Advances in the understanding of pathology and disease transmission, coupled with those in physical and biological sciences, provided spectacular cures for a wide range of conditions. Here the practitioners' desire was to display their mastery of disease and its treatment, perhaps in the face of ignorance and doubt on the part of their patients. Bedside manner was no longer crucial, so long as the patient took the medicine and followed the doctor's orders, for the 'doctor knew best'. The era of the 'pill for every ill' began with great promise, but the result was to increase the knowledge gap between practitioners and their clients. This brought a startling change to the balance of power and control: the health worker, especially the medical practitioner, began to assume a very central position. Other actors, family and community members, were pushed out to the margins, their influence undermined by the new advances.

A gradual sense of disenchantment and frustration set in as the limitations of scientific medicine became clearer: resistant strains of infectious agents; adverse reactions to drugs; the failure to resolve common and urgent problems. While the doctor might know best, he or she did not seem to know enough. Eventually this led to a thorough review of health-care provision and the optimum mechanism for achieving good health across the whole population. While high-technology medicine had claimed centre-stage with its dramatic gains, the failure to address other issues remained a serious concern. The eradication of smallpox proved to be a peak of achievement which has not since been matched. Malaria, diarrhoea, pneumonia, and malnutrition all continued to take a high toll of human life. Attention turned to the need to expand health care beyond the limitations of the medical model, as changing perspectives brought different issues to the centre of the debate.

Primary Health Care, as envisaged at the 1978 Alma Ata conference, attempted to reorient the provision of health care towards an holistic, preventative approach.[2] It stressed the social, economic, and political aspects of health and disease, emphasising the need for inter-sectoral work and collaboration. This was an effort to expand the focus and responsibility for health from the medical professions to a far broader base, to some degree returning to an aspect of earlier times in which care and cure were obtained locally from personally known practitioners. Given the radical nature of this reorientation, it is not surprising that it met with resistance and proved to be a much more complex task than was initially realised. The struggle continues, with new manifestations of PHC appearing in the form of 'community based health care', 'integrated health and development projects', and similar approaches emphasising participation, empowerment, and decentralisation.

The cyclical nature of the movement from centre to margin and back again is clear, although there is no straightforward return to a past situation, rather a re-emergence of issues and concerns in new forms. The re-emergence of an emphasis on the social nature of health and the importance of social-support networks in health maintenance which came with PHC exposed a number of dilemmas.

Participation

Within this new context the practitioner appears as a guide, someone with specific technical knowledge which is put at the service of the needs of the community. The distance between practitioners and clients is reduced again, as practitioners attempt to explain their understanding in terms which non-professionals can understand, and to adjust their priorities to those of the community around them. The pre-eminence of the practitioner is undermined still further, as efforts are made to (re)learn more about non-allopathic approaches and local understanding of the means to achieve health and prevent illness. In this context, practitioners feel themselves being pushed out to the margin as the centrality of their contribution is challenged. Having held such a central position for a considerable period of time, many are uneasy at letting go of the reins.

There is also the challenge of finding a successful mechanism through which community participation can be achieved. A great deal of effort has gone into the study of

this. Health practitioners have learned skills in group dynamics, conflict resolution, team building, and community development in order that they may foster effective participation. At the local level in a large variety of contexts a measure of success has been achieved, for which the reward has also been great. Provision of health care has become a joint endeavour between all sections of a community, with each person making his or her own contribution to the whole, however small. Recognition of the value of differing contributions is now widespread. This process can be viewed as another example of the way in which various aspects of life continually move from marginal to central positions. Health is often of marginal interest to the majority of community members: a concern only when it deserts them and they fall sick. Where participation is fostered, the centrality of good health to a productive life is recognised and acted upon. Health becomes the hub at the centre of the wheel, holding everything together and allowing movement in the desired direction.

An additional benefit of this process is the way in which it builds trust between health workers and community members. This narrows the gap which the training of professional health workers may create between them and the population they serve. Practitioners come to recognise the importance of other actors in maintaining health and the value of their knowledge. An example is the work of SARTHI in Gujarat, India.[3] While attempting to improve health-care provision in the area, project workers realised that herbal medicine played a vital role in local practice. Rather than dismissing this as old fashioned or irrelevant, the project took an active role in discovering precisely how these herbal remedies worked and which conditions they could be used to combat. Unsurprisingly many of the traditional remedies proved to be effective against exactly the conditions for which they had always been prescribed. The result was an active encouragement of herbal gardens as a widely available and affordable health resource. A tradition which had been marginalised by the success of allopathic medicine was reclaimed. More importantly it remained firmly in the hands of the local population, who therefore kept a central role in their own health care.

Funding and bureaucracy

Fostering the participation of the community is one challenge. It is quite another to integrate the contributions and programmes of different departments or sectors into efforts to attain overall health goals. One of the most serious barriers to this is the nature of departmental budgets and financial structures. Within the bureaucratic structures of governments, it is necessary to maintain strict lines of authority and accountability. Money is allocated to achieve specific ends dictated by the priorities of the department. When staff from different departments try to combine their activities or create joint work programmes, negotiating the budgetary freedom to enable this to occur can be difficult. To which department will costs be allocated for transport, for joint workshops, for programme administration? Can all this be justified? How will differing priorities be reconciled? Who will be in charge overall (and who will thereby feel pushed to the margins)? In a project to promote good nutrition through increased agricultural production of nutritious food, does the health department or the agriculture department take charge? These are not idle questions, and while 'common sense' may lead us to the conclusion that the responsibility must be shared, this is not easy to achieve administratively.

A further layer of complexity is added by the influence of those agencies which provide the funds for health care. Application deadlines must be met. Funding is for time-limited periods only. Hard evidence of the positive outcomes of past funding is required when applying for future funds. Each agency has its own agenda to promote. Certain activities are highly favoured and

others less so, and this quite naturally changes over time. For those attempting to provide services over a sustained period of time, the prospect of failing to obtain funding is a very real one. The changing fashions within the health and development scene do not always work in their favour. Environment, population, gender awareness, urbanisation, responding to HIV, eradication of polio: these are just a few of the fashionable issues of recent years. All of them are important and should not be ignored, but many projects are mainly concerned with the continued provision of basic health care. Valuable time and energy are squandered as staff try to fit their proposals to the latest fad. Another current favourite is sustainability. Not only is this hard to define; it may also be unrealistic: can the poorest countries or regions ever hope to rely only on their own resources? After all, it is not the case that developed countries do so; rather they draw on many resources worldwide. Of course, sustainability is not merely a financial concept. It has other dimensions which are equally important: cultural, environmental, organisational, political, and social.

The economic margin and equity

Perhaps the most pervasive of recent fashions is that in which health is viewed from a predominantly economic perspective, with cost-effectiveness and value-for-money taking priority. The reform movement sweeping through public administration and economic structural adjustment have made a significant impact on the thinking of health-care policy-makers. The terminology has changed again to *costs, inputs, products, efficiency* and (less often) *investment*. A by-product of this most recent shift has been that funding proposals for health-related activities are increasingly being designed with these economic parameters in mind. The way in which this can potentially distort the project objectives and activities is open to debate, but there is no doubt that it is proving very difficult to translate health into purely economic terms. The costs of treatment or illness are slightly easier to estimate, but the benefits of health to an individual remain hard to quantify in monetary terms. Practitioners become caught in the tension between economic calculation of general costs and benefits and provision of humane care to individuals in specific need. It is a tension which many find impossible to resolve.

Once again it is important to analyse how this new focus changes the centre and the margins within the field of health care. Assessment of health benefits in economic terms means that the importance of those who are economically inactive or invisible is reduced. It also undermines the value of other contributions to health and well-being which may be of a social or psychological nature. I am thinking of an older woman I knew in Papua New Guinea. She did not perform any visible economic activity, being old and weak. On the surface she consumed rather than produced resources; thus there was little incentive to expend still more on maintaining her health. But what of the value of her knowledge and wisdom in the resolution of family or community conflicts? What of her value in the education of the children through myths, storytelling, and personal history? What of her knowledge of herbal and household remedies for common illnesses? How to assess in monetary terms the fact that she can call upon the support of other community members in times of hardship, just as she has assisted them in times past? These are vital contributions to the continued health of her community, but we have a long way to go before we can cost them. Too often the economic spotlight is turned upon the more straightforward task of assessing the cost of treating her arthritis or her chronic obstructive lung disease: inevitably, she shows up as a negative item on the balance sheet.

Another variant of the economic argument is that of the neo-liberalist, urging us towards privatisation of service provision. While there may be some advantages to this, it is highly unlikely that they will accrue to those on the margins of a society. Of necessity, private investors are interested in profit and will concentrate their provision where the highest profit margin can be gained. Governments may reduce State provision as private-sector efforts increase, especially when financial constraints operate, using the argument that their provision is no longer needed, as the private sector has taken over this responsibility. However, the net result is usually that services for the better-off multiply, while those for the poor are undermined still further.

This pattern is in danger of being repeated on far too large a scale if the supremacy of economics continues unchallenged. Health and welfare services are cut back with the argument that they are not cost-effective. Money is diverted into production of goods for export in order to boost the economic growth of the country. That this is a short-sighted option may at last be becoming apparent to its promoters, who have previously been dazzled by the sparkle of the *nouveaux riches* which it has created. Poorly fed, poorly educated, unfit people do not make for a prosperous nation. Evidence is growing that health is strongly affected by social divisions. Death rates are higher in societies with the greatest gaps between rich and poor. The well-known health risks of being poor are greatly increased if we know that our neighbour is rich. Social and economic inequality do not promote good health, though they may create large profits for multinational corporations.

Compelling evidence of this comes most clearly from the developed rather than the developing countries. In the United States and the United Kingdom, the health of the poorest has been declining, despite increased expenditure on health care and despite economic growth. For the UK, general health was best during times of national crisis: the major world wars of this century. Great efforts were made to ensure that everyone had the basic necessities for life (through a rationing system), while at the same time the vital importance of everyone's contribution to the war effort was strongly emphasised. Divisions were minimised and equitable sharing of the burdens stressed, with very real benefits for health. It is sad that it seems possible to achieve this level of cohesion only in the face of an enemy, for in all other ways war is undoubtedly the greatest of health hazards. Indeed, the difficulties of health-care provision at times of armed conflict or in its aftermath are one of the major preoccupations of the present time.

Conclusion

It is easy to be cynical about the way in which we provide for the health of those living at the margins of our society. We seem to make most demands of those with least resources. It is those currently without care who are asked to build their own facilities, fund the services they require, and manage them in a gender-fair and disability-friendly manner. The demand for sustainability is made of those living in the most precarious of situations. Meanwhile those with already existing health facilities continue to manage and use them as before. But change comes in two ways: as a revolution or as a gradual process. Given the nature of health-care provision which relies on many well-established institutions and a large, often centrally trained workforce, revolution is unlikely. This leaves us with the option of a gradual process. It is at the margins of the health system that movement and change are most possible. It is where the system is not working that we are most likely to try out new ideas. It is those who are currently not included who can tell us most clearly what is needed to reach them. It is in this context that principles of participation, empowerment, and equity become such potent forces for positive change, through the way in which they shift the locus of control and redefine both centre and margin.

'Health for all' is by now a well-worn slogan and the target date of the year 2000 no longer realistic. But it is a slogan which neatly summarises much of the foregoing argument for concentration on the needs of those at the margins. If we have the courage to learn from what occurs at the margins and apply these lessons to the overall system, then — although we may never reach every marginal group — I believe we will move a long way towards a fully inclusive health-care system.

Notes

1 The terms *margin* and *marginalisation* are used here to indicate those people, ideas, or places which are left out or excluded from mainstream policy and practice. The concept of *exclusion* has the same meaning.

2 PHC as a strategy is based on a few fundamental principles, often referred to as the pillars of PHC. These are equity, participation, and intersectoral collaboration. The emphases on prevention and the development and use of appropriate technology are also central to the approach. Equity requires that efforts are directed at those most in need, in order to reduce any existing inequalities in health. It is not simple equality in which everyone receives exactly the same, but a deliberate redistribution of resources towards those who have least. Participation is valued in all aspects of health and health care — planning, prioritising, implementing, and evaluating — and by all groups of people. These two principles in particular have implications for the health of those currently at the margins of any society. Intersectoral collaboration requires that the efforts of all government and non-government agencies be directed towards the improvement of health for the population as a whole. Integration of policies and practical activities to maximise health is the intended result.

3 R. Khannu (1992): 'Taking Charge: Women's Health as Empowerment — The SARTHI Experience', SAHAJ/SARTHI.

Research on women's health:
some methodological issues

T. K. Sundari Ravindran

Introduction

This article concerns research on issues related to women's health, and particularly *applied* research falling within the purview of health systems, as opposed to clinical or bio-medical investigation. Research into health systems concerns itself with all the relevant variables — social, economic, political, and cultural — that may influence the health status of a population and their health-seeking behaviour. It thus addresses broader issues than the planning, organisation, and delivery of services. It is important, because, for many crucial problems today, valid scientific knowledge is available. What seems to be difficult is the application of this knowledge for the well-being of all sections of the population.

There are several reasons why it is important to focus on women's health.

- Health problems requiring priority care are different for men and women.

- Factors leading to ill-health vary according to sex. This is explained not only by reproductive morbidity and mortality. The sexual division of labour means that men and women do different tasks, and are exposed differentially to various risk factors and agents causing illness. For example, within the household women usually bear greater responsibility than men for cooking, waste disposal, and working with water. There are differences in the nature of work done outside the house as well. Furthermore, in most societies women are frequently victims of violence, both domestic and sexual, physical and psychological.

- There is limited knowledge about even some of the most basic health problems of women, such as those relating to menstruation and various infections of the reproductive tract; not to mention psychosocial and mental-health problems.

- One of the most telling examples of failure to apply existing scientific knowledge to improving women's health status relates to maternal mortality, which in developing countries is 50 times higher than in industrialised countries — a figure which indicates the extent of preventable female mortality in poor societies.

- One of the least-studied areas relates to women's participation in solving their own health problems, although theoretically this ought to have been a focal part of studies of community involvement.

We need to know more about various aspects of women's health, and in particular we need answers to the following questions:

- What problems do women from different social groups experience?
- What are the causal factors?
- What are women's perceptions, and what is their understanding of their problems?

- What are the factors influencing their health-seeking behaviour?
- How can women be enabled or empowered to participate in solving their own health problems?

A framework for analysing women's health status

A given methodology is as good or as limited as one's framework of analysis. This is illustrated by the story of the factory whose machinery caused serious injuries to its workers, and the nature of the responses to the problem (see Box).[1] The 'problems' that a research team identifies and the 'solutions' that it proposes depend very much on a particular world view: what the researchers see as 'given', and the parameters within which they function.

Our framework for analysing issues concerning women's health is given in Figure 1. As can be seen, the components we have identified are inter-related. Variables include both those that influence women's susceptibility to illness, and those that influence their response to ill health.

There was once a factory which employed thousands of people. Its production was a miracle of modern engineering, turning out thousands of machines every day. The factory had a high accident rate. The complicated machinery of the production line took little account of human error, forgetfulness, or ignorance. Day after day men and women came out of it with squashed fingers, cuts, bruises. Sometimes a man would lose an arm or leg. Occasionally someone was electrocuted or crushed to death.

Enlightened people began to see that something needed to be done. First on the scene were the churches. An enterprising minister organised a small first-aid tent outside the factory gate. Soon, with the backing of the Council of Churches, it grew into a properly built clinic, able to give first aid to quite serious cases, and to treat minor injuries. The Town Council became interested, together with local bodies like the Chamber of Trade and the Rotary Club. The clinic grew into a small hospital, with modern equipment, an operating theatre, and a full-time staff of doctors and nurses. Several lives were saved. Finally the factory management, seeing the good that was being done, and wishing to prove itself enlightened, gave the hospital its official backing, with unrestricted access to the factory, a small annual grant, and an ambulance to speed serious cases from the workshop to hospital ward.

But year by year, as production increased, the accident rate continued to rise. More and more men and women were hurt or maimed. And, in spite of everything the hospital could do, more people died from the injuries they received.

Concerned and influential individuals in the local community therefore advised the factory management to call in a consultant for advice on how to reduce accident rates. The consultant pointed out that the management had thus far neglected accident prevention, and prevailed upon them to organise a workshop for workers about occupational safety. This had an immediate positive impact; but, after about a year, accident rates returned to the original levels. A second consultant advised that workers above the age of 40 should not be retained on the production line, because their reflexes were slow and they were the most accident-prone.

Nobody in all this time ever questioned why the factory had to have high-productivity machines at such a cost to workers' health.[1]

Figure 1: A framework for analysis of issues related to women and health

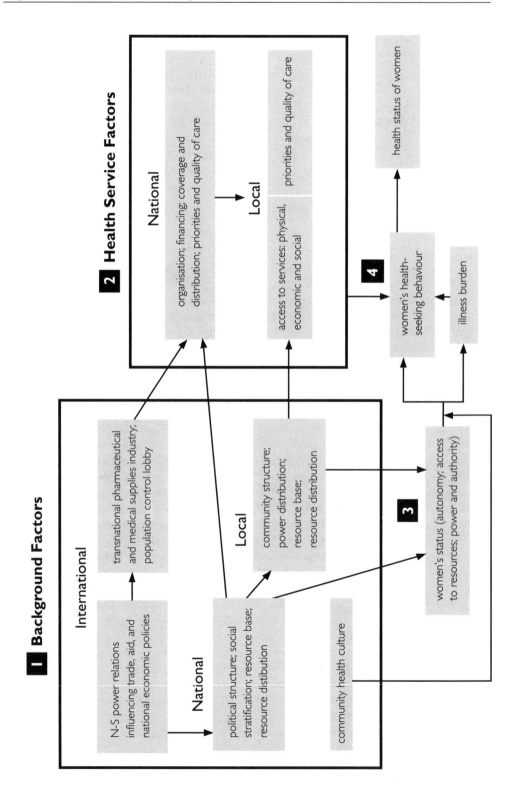

We start from the premise that disease is a natural/biological reality which is both socially produced and socially defined, and influenced by the global and local economic environment. We also see it as resulting from a process of interaction between these various factors which are themselves changing and evolving, both as individual entities and as interconnected sub-systems. Our framework consists essentially of four major components.

- *Background factors:* the socio-political context which influences people's economic environment and well-being, the characteristics of health-service systems, and women's status in the society.

- *Health-service factors:* how services are financed (with State funding or as part of the market economy), who controls them, their priorities, coverage, and distribution, and the quality of care provided.

- *Women's status:* itself the product of a number of variables included in background factors, but an important determinant with respect to women's health status.

- *Women's perceptions of health and illness, and their health-seeking behaviour:* again, determined by the interaction between background factors and community health culture; women's status and health-service factors.

Background factors

We have considered background factors in two tiers, consisting of the macro and micro dimensions respectively. The macro dimension looks into factors which influence conditions at a national level, while the micro dimension is concerned with factors influencing health status within a community, and accounting for differentials in health status within it and between one community and another.

Given the transnationalisation of commerce and production, and the inter-dependence of economies across the globe, the macro-dimension needs to take into consideration influences of the world economy on the economy of a nation. A recent work on the influence of world recession on child welfare develops a comprehensive picture of macro-factors and their systemic inter-relationships.[2]

Our framework also incorporates the pharmaceutical industry and the population-control establishment, both of which have considerable influence on national health-service systems. We have added a second tier, namely factors influencing health status at the community level. This is to make allowances for inter-community and intra-community differentials in the enjoyment of good health and exposure to the risk of disease.

Two major components within micro-factors have been identified: (a) the characteristics of the community to which women belong; and (b) the health culture of the community.

The first set includes the social divisions within the community: caste, race, ethnicity, for instance; then the availability of material and non-material resources: the size of the cake at its disposal; and finally the distribution of these resources across the various sub-divisions of society already identified. For example, women may be affected because they belong to a very poor sub-section, such as a poor caste or a group of landless labourers. Alternatively, although they belong to a wealthy rich sub-group or a relatively rich community, they may be affected by discrimination. Or, as is usually the case, women may suffer as a consequence of both poverty and discrimination. Each must be differentiated, since each requires different strategies for action.

By a community's health culture, we mean attitudes to health and illness, and to fertility and its control; beliefs about the etiology of various health problems; traditional healing resources commonly used; and the community's attitude to formal health services. Practices and beliefs concerning menstruation, pregnancy, and childbirth would feature prominently among these.

Health-service factors

Health-service factors have also been considered at the macro and micro levels. National health-service systems are influenced directly by international factors such as the transnational pharmaceutical industry and the population-control establishment; and indirectly (through its influence on the national economy) by the international economic climate as a whole. They invariably reflect the character of the national economy — whether State-funded and subsidised, marketed by the private sector as a service with a price, or consisting of both private and public sectors, as the case may be.

At the micro level these factors relate to the resource base and power base of the community in question. An urban community or a wealthy social group thus has better access in general, as well as access to enhanced quality and more appropriate services, than does a poor or a socially marginalised community.

Women's status

Women's susceptibility to illness is necessarily a product of their status within their communities, irrespective of the social group to which they belong. Thus, besides income and educational level, indicators of women's status would also include social indicators, for example their level of autonomy and physical mobility, and the incidence of male violence against them. Mechanisms for women's participation in decision-making are also an indicator of women's status. Are there groups of women, formal or informal, in which they can come together and discuss their health needs, or put pressure on the authorities? Is there a place for women in decision-making bodies in the local government or village councils, through which they can express their needs and make demands?

Women's perceptions of illness, and their health-seeking behaviour

This is the fourth major influence on women's health, and is itself mediated by a number of the factors and variables already discussed. Women's status, the health culture of the community, and health-service factors interact in the process whereby women decide what to do when they get sick.

A woman's status affects her self-perception about whether she deserves to take care of herself or not. In some cultures (like the one I belong to), a woman is not expected to complain. A woman would feel that she has failed as a woman if she could not cope: 'Everybody else seems to be doing it. What's wrong with me?'

Again, for certain kinds of illness or for certain kinds of health event, it is not usual for members of the community to seek medical help. Since pregnancy is a normal event, why go for antenatal care? This has more to do with the community's beliefs about health than with women's status *per se*. The numerous beliefs and practices surrounding menstruation, pregnancy, and childbirth, as well as attitudes to fertility and its control, which are part of the community's health culture specifically affect both women's health and their health-seeking behaviour.

Health-service factors also exert great influence: physical as well as social accessibility, affordability of services in terms of monetary and other costs, and quality of care.

We have presented a long list of factors that may influence women's health. Some of these influence women's susceptibility to illness, while the others influence their health-seeking behaviour. It is not that every single one needs to be taken into account in any given study. Rather, what we have presented is a framework for analysis, presenting variables to be taken into account as impinging on women's health.

Methods of enquiry

The appropriate research methodology depends on the specific purpose of the study in question. There may be very simple ways of investigating certain questions, while for others we may need sophisticated techniques. Facts are only as sacred as the use to which they are put. We need not be obsessed with being able to produce quantitative data correct to the last decimal point.

Through a combination of qualitative methods and better-known techniques for the collection of quantitative data, and the use of existing secondary data, one can gather information related to various components of the framework described above. However, the methodologies discussed in this article are related to only one aspect: namely, the collection of primary information from the field. These are probably not standard data-collection methods, but we present them here in the light of having used them in community-based research. All but one relate to the collection of *qualitative* information. We also describe one example of doing a large-scale health-interview survey with community involvement.

The methodologies described below have been useful in gathering information to help to assess health needs, to understand factors influencing ill health in a given community, and to learn about perceptions and attitudes that affect health. (These methodologies can be employed for any exercise in primary data collection, and are not specific to research on women's health.)

Community-based research often ends up investigating what outsiders need to know about what insiders in the community already know. In fact, the need

may be not to gather more information, but to gather everyone together to look at what they already know. This, then, is a basic starting principle.

Observation

Observation can yield worthwhile results and can be an unobtrusive way of learning. It can be a very good exercise for an outsider entering a community for the first time, just to watch and observe before shooting off questions. Effective observation demands that the outsider has a clear idea of what she or he wants to observe. This is why we emphasised the framework in the beginning.

Observation can, for example, give information about the community's physical resources; social groupings and settlement patterns; activities that people engage in; and differences in living and working conditions across social groups. It can reveal where and how women spend their time, how they are treated, how healthy or otherwise they look; whether there is a visible distinction in the ways that boys and girls are treated ... and so on.

This is, of course, only a first step, a stage in which to formulate questions needing further probing, or hypotheses for testing on a wider scale.

Group interviews

Group interviews may take place in informal or formal settings. There are several situations when people gather informally — in somebody's courtyard, in somebody's workplace — and they can be useful opportunities to find out more about situations applicable to the community as a whole. What is the work season? How many people get work in general? What are the wage levels? Are wages different for men and women? For answers to many questions there is no need to go house to house. One can get a general picture from an informal group interview. A household survey is necessary only if more refined information is needed.

More formal group interviews take place in settings such as workshops, and are especially useful for research related to women's health. In a workshop setting, groups of women are able to respond to sensitive questions better than when interviewed at home, where they may be reluctant to talk with men or elders around. Formal group interviews are also useful when women need to be presented with some facts before questions can be posed. For example, we held a workshop discussion on symptoms of gynaecological infections. There were many questions and requests for clarification from the women. To ask them, 'Have you ever had such symptoms before?' was then much easier. But in a household morbidity survey where you start off asking for symptoms, women may often not know what you are talking about, or may not feel free to share their health problems.

The author has also used formal group interviews to gain a sense of the extent and major causes of infant death. When we asked the group, 'How many of you have lost a baby?' and everyone had, we did not have to calculate the infant mortality rate in that community to know that something was terribly wrong. For our purposes, this was enough:

> 'What did they die of?'
> 'Oh, we don't know.'
> 'Did they die immediately after birth?'
> 'Yes.'and so on.

We discovered that many were neonatal deaths, and that they were not related to neonatal tetanus. They seemed more related to the women's health problems during pregnancy, such as hypertensive disorders, and to difficulties during labour.

Talking to key respondents

This is a method often used by social scientists and anthropologists. It is useful to talk to key people in the different social groups within the community, rather than treating the community as a homogeneous entity.

The same question may have to be asked of people who you think may have different perspectives — those from different age groups, for example, or different power centres — to avoid getting a one-sided and partial picture. For example, we talked to the public-health nurse and the medical officer in charge of the health centre, to assess their views on what the community needed most, and why services were not delivered or utilised as planned. And then we talked to some women in the community to find out what they thought. This helped us to gain a grasp of varied and conflicting perceptions, and to identify areas for remedial action. Talking to key people is also useful for gathering specialised information: we spoke with traditional birth attendants, for example, to find out about birth practices; and with the village headman to learn about relevant State-funded development programmes.

Collecting case studies

Case-study collection is useful if, for example, we are interested in identifying multiple causes leading to a death, disability, or serious illness. In the case of maternal mortality, a woman may have died of haemorrhage during labour; but there are many other factors, such as her being poor, multiparous, distant from health facilities, and so on which, in conjunction, were responsible for her death. Case-study collections have helped to identify a number of non-medical variables that may make the essential difference between life and death.

Role-play and drama techniques

Another method which we have found valuable is role-playing by women in the community. This is best organised in a workshop setting, as in the case of formal group interviews. This is very useful with women's groups who are not used to standing up and expressing their ideas and thoughts. But when you ask: 'Can you portray what happened when such and such a woman fell seriously ill in your village?', they get together and enact the situation with relative ease. And through their portrayal we learn about many of the processes that cause a particular illness, and the decision-making processes that determine whether or not medical help is sought. The woman falls ill, and then you see the role-players asking so-and-so before they make decisions about what to do; and they perform particular rituals, prepare certain home remedies, and so on. We would never have found out about them by asking questions, because we would not have been aware that such variables existed.

Health interview surveys

We describe below an example of an attempt to do a large-scale survey of reproductive morbidity in women. It was undertaken by a rural women's organisation, which selected a group of women from the community who had been trained over the previous couple of years as basic health promoters. They were aware of some of the major health problems of women and children, and could recognise the symptoms. They knew how to treat them with local cures and simple drugs, and to identify when medical help was necessary.

A workshop was organised for these women, explaining the need for systematic data collection, and involving them in drawing up a questionnaire concerning women's pregnancy histories and symptoms of health problems. A second workshop was organised after a trial run of the questionnaire in one community, in which doubts and difficulties were clarified. Questionnaires were checked, and incorrect or incomplete entries were pointed out.

The women then started the survey. It was not a sample survey, but a complete enumeration of all the households in the lower-caste settlements of 48 villages, a total of 3,000 households. A baseline survey was done, and the morbidity profile was updated every month. The researchers then rechecked a 10 per cent sample of completed questionnaires in every village, using house visits. When we found major discrepancies, the entire settlement was resurveyed by a group made up of researcher/health promoters from other villages, to ensure that data were not falsified once again.

To eliminate recall errors, we asked questions pertaining only to current illness: what symptoms the respondent was suffering from on the day of the interview. We had a checklist of symptoms related to common reproductive health problems in the area and went through it, instead of just asking the women if they were sick. In order to reconfirm that symptoms reported did in fact correspond to the health problems they were presumed to denote, we once again relied on a 10 per cent sample of the women who had been studied. A clinical examination was carried out by a gynaecologist on this sample of women, to give an idea of margins of error and errors specific to certain health problems. We subsequently modified the questionnaire and our methods for the next round. We did this over one year, and by the end of this process we had evolved a fairly trustworthy procedure.

Such a survey has had several advantages: we have gathered sufficient data at a relatively low cost. The extent of morbidity may be higher than we have identified, but we definitely know that the prevalence rates are at least 33 per cent in our case. A clinical examination of a large sample would be ideal, but, since it would also be very expensive, it would never get done. We also know what the major health problems are, how women interpret their etiology, and so on.

More important, however, is the fact that the survey results are not just sitting in a computer's memory. Women in the community are very much more aware now of their own health problems. Women who have been trained as health promoters now know more clearly the nature of the local problems, and are more effective in treating them. We have tried to summarise the results in pictorial form, and have held exhibitions in the villages where we collected the data. These have stimulated considerable discussion: 'This many women complained of this and this. This many women went to the health services, and this many didn't go. Why?' We have also had role-plays enacted by health promoters, depicting local case-studies, to provoke discussion about all the ways in which a death or disability could have been prevented, the identity of the different actors, and the courses of action open to them. Even large-scale surveys can thus be actively used as tools for education and awareness-raising, and as a way of bringing about local participation in solving people's own health problems.

One further point about the qualitative methods described above: these methods can be used even in conventional research where quantitative accuracy is important, as part of an exploratory phase to get a better sense of the variables involved, or in an attempt to understand puzzling results. This holds true whether the research involves primary data collection or whether it draws on secondary data sources. To give an example, we discovered on analysing data from our health interview survey that newly married young women received no medical help whatsoever when they developed reproductive health problems. On being asked why, they replied that they were afraid. The group interview process revealed that these women were virtually powerless within their marital homes, not having yet provided progeny to carry on the family name. They feared that if they fell ill, they would be considered a liability and sent back to their parental homes.

It is clear from the methodologies described above that it does not require 'specialists' to carry out research on women's health. All it requires is the willingness and commitment to start with an open mind, and learn from ordinary people. Our task is to challenge the specialists' monopoly over information on what ails women; and to generate information on women's health from the life experiences and perceptions of affected women — information that takes into consideration women's whole selves and circumstances.

Notes

1 A modified version of 'The modern parable' from *It's Not Fair*, written and compiled by Anne Wilkinson, Christian Aid, London, 1985.
2 Giovanni Andrea Cornia: 'A summary and interpretation of the evidence', *World Development* 12(3), pp. 381-91, 1984.

The author

T. K. Sundari Ravindran is a founding member of Rural Women's Social Education Centre, Tamil Nadu. She has worked as co-editor of the newsletter of the Women's Global Network for Reproductive Rights. This article is based on a paper delivered by the author at the National Symposium on Women and Health in Developing Countries, San José de Costa Rica, 4-6 June 1991. It was first published in *Development in Practice* in Volume 2, Number 3, in 1992.

Deterrents to immunisation in Somalia:
a survey of mothers' attitudes

Anne LaFond

Introduction

Throughout the 1980s, international health planners argued that increased access to immunisation would rapidly reduce high rates of mortality among children. By 1985, when the worldwide goal of Universal Child Immunisation by 1990 (UCI 90) was set, many health-sector development strategies focused on increasing immunisation coverage. Most Southern governments and inter-national donors declared their commitment to achieving UCI 90, and pledged their resources accordingly. By the end of the decade, reported figures for immunisation coverage from around the world were tallied; and, at the World Summit for Children, held in September 1990, Universal Child Immunisation was at last declared.

Unfortunately, global figures tend to mask the less successful experiences. Few reports have emerged from those countries which failed to achieve the UCI 90 goal. Nor have we learned the reason why these programmes might have failed. Like many countries, Somalia joined the immunisation `band wagon', launching its national pro-gramme with great political zeal. In the latter half of the decade, access to immu-nisation improved rapidly. Nevertheless, ten years after the programme began, many mothers remained sceptical of this particular health intervention. Their reservations were expressed as some of the lowest national coverage figures in the world.

Little was known about women's reasons for not accepting immunisation. While poor access to health facilities compounded low coverage, even where immunisation was available, demand remained low. Previous attempts to investigate the reasons for non-completion of immunisation in Somalia revealed a wide range of explanations. However, few studies were able to determine the relative influence of different factors on people's acceptance of the schemes. (See Mohammed 1986 and Ministry of Health 1988.)

To assess the reasons for low demand, the national Expanded Programme on Immunisation (EPI) and Save the Children Fund (UK) jointly embarked on a community-based study of immunisation acceptability. The research aimed to assess individual and collective experience with the programme, to ascertain the reasons for poor acceptance, and so determine practical ways to improve uptake. However, the research also conveyed to programme managers an entire history of immunisation at grassroots level. Members of the community were able to explain, in their own words, the role which they played in the drive for Universal Child Immunisation.

Background

Somalia is a country of only 8 million inhabitants. It is estimated that more than half the population live a nomadic or seminomadic existence. Although the country is linguistically uniform, Somali became a written language only in 1972. Education levels are poor, and much of the population remains illiterate. Poor communication networks, remote and migrating communities, plus a moribund health system all tend to frustrate the consistent delivery of health care and health information.

Before the overthrow of President Siad Barre in January 1991, the Somali Socialist Revolutionary Party played a pivotal role in political and 'official' social life in the country. Party workers, representing various sectors — youth, labour, health, politics, and agriculture — were assigned to each administrative division of every village and town. The government normally employed them to organise political activities and to provide a focal point in the community for national development programmes, including immunisation.

The immunisation programme

In 1978 the government launched the Expanded Programme on Immunisation, introducing immunisation for women and children in Banadir Region, which included the capital, Mogadishu. The programme aimed to immunise 80 per cent of all children aged 11–23 months against six killer diseases (polio, diphtheria, whooping cough, tetanus, tuberculosis, and measles), as well as 75 per cent of all women of child-bearing age to prevent tetanus in new-borns. Activity increased slowly from 1978 to 1985, when three successive immunisation campaigns were held throughout the country. A number of international development agencies actively supported this initiative, providing substantial resources to assist the Somali government in meeting campaign targets.

By enlisting a network of Party officials and workers, all women of child-bearing age and all under-fives were registered and taken to specified centres to receive immunisation. Information was disseminated at community level through Party cadres, many of whom had little or no previous knowledge of immunisation. Measures used by the government to ensure compliance during the campaigns were often extreme. Mothers refusing immunisation were threatened with fines or imprisonment; some were forcibly taken to the immunisation site. Health staff, instructed to meet targets, also placed pressure on women and would actively seek out children whose mothers failed to attend. At this time, many health workers were trained to administer vaccines and gained a basic, but limited, understanding of immunisation and health-education messages. While 'community' mobilisation was generally effective, immunisation sites were often crowded and chaotic. Achieving high coverage often took precedence over genuine and effective patient care.

In most cases, the campaigns succeeded in raising coverage dramatically. Nevertheless within a year, rates fell as new cohorts of eligible children failed to come forward for immunisation. In response, the government initiated a second strategy, opening many new sites in most major towns. Situated in Party Orientation Centres, and staffed with more newly-trained nurses, these services aimed to bring immunisation closer to the grassroots and to encourage Party cadres to mobilise the mothers. Concurrent efforts to raise awareness included radio broadcasts, drama productions, 'Mobilisation Days', and a birth-registration programme.

From 1985 to 1988, Somalis watched immunisation activities achieve national importance. However, despite these efforts to secure coverage targets, actual demand remained low. In 1989, among children in Mogadishu, where access was greatest, coverage of DPT3 (the third and final dose of a trivalent vaccine for diphtheria, polio, and tetanus) was only 25 per cent; and only 26 per cent of eligible women had received at least two doses of tetanus vaccine.

Research objectives and approach

The objectives of this research were two-fold:

- to gain understanding of health-seeking behaviour among Somali mothers, and thereby determine the factors influencing the acceptance of immunisation;

- to make recommendations for improving acceptance, in order to increase the use made of immunisation services.

Since the research aimed to discover the attitudes and beliefs contributing to low demand, researchers took a qualitative approach to data-gathering. Previous studies to assess poor acceptance used closed questionnaires as an adjunct to coverage surveys; and no fewer than 15 different reasons for incomplete immunisation emerged. Although they offered some insight, quantitative methods had failed either to determine the relative importance of the different factors or to clarify the relationship between them. An open-ended, qualitative approach allowed for variables to arise from the research and then be explored thoroughly. Potential sensitivity to some research topics also influenced our choice of methods. The immunisation programme had clear links with political goals and Party activities. It was assumed, therefore, that some respondents would be loath to speak candidly and critically in response to direct questions about a government programme.

Site selection

One urban community (Yaqshiid district, Mogadishu) and one rural community (Jamame district, Lower Juba Region) were selected for the study. Criteria for selection included the presence of a functioning Mother and Child Health (MCH) centre, relatively consistent availability of immunisation for at least one year, and the presence of related outreach activities.

Data-gathering focused on the catchment areas of both MCH centres. However, in Jamame, two additional settlements were included in the study to assess the extent of awareness of immunisation in communities which did not have access to health services and formal immunisation promotion. The latter were also selected to provide better understanding of perceptions concerning disease and concepts of prevention. Before the data were gathered, immunisation coverage was measured in Yaqshiid district, using a standard WHO 30 cluster survey. Current coverage rates in Jamame district were already available, and so no survey was conducted. Coverage of three doses of DPT vaccine in Yaqshiid and Jamame measured 25 per cent and 34 per cent respectively.

Methods

Data were derived through three methods:

- focus-group discussions with mothers assembled by age and parity;
- informal interviews with individuals associated directly with the immunisation programme, and those identified as sources of health advice in the community;
- observation of official and traditional health practices.

Women selected for focus groups represented all the administrative areas of each community. They were grouped according to age and parity, reflecting local perceptions of experience and authority in relation to child-rearing. It was felt that respect for older, more experienced women would hinder discussion if mothers of all ages were grouped together. Groups consisted of women aged 16–30 with fewer than four children; women aged 31–45 with four or more children; and mothers who had completed child-bearing. Discussions took place in the home of a group member, and lasted from one to three hours.

Informal individual interviews were undertaken to complement discussion data and provide a wider perspective of local experience with immunisation and health care. Respondents included officials associated with the immunisation programme: government and party leaders and health staff; and community members identified through focus groups as 'health advisers': traditional and religious healers, knowledgeable older women, and midwives.

To assess the relationship between mothers and health providers and the effectiveness of immunisation messages, researchers observed activities in MCH centres, immunisation sites, and treatment sessions run by traditional and religious healers.

The research team consisted of one expatriate and two Somali researchers. Researchers lived in each study site for one month, often within households or families. All interviews and discussions were carried out in Somali and reviewed, discussed, and written up on the day of the interview. The following topics were used to guide the research:

- awareness and knowledge of immunisation;
- attitudes towards characteristics of immunisation: safety, effectiveness, accessibility, and cost;
- perceptions of diseases preventable by vaccine;
- perceptions and practices related to prevention;
- perceptions of methods of promoting and delivering immunisation;
- the role of health advice in the community.

Results

First impressions

When the Ministry of Health introduced immunisation through national campaigns, government and health personnel were held responsible for ensuring that all women and children were registered and immunised. This first thrust for high coverage set the stage for the future of the programme. Experiences reported during the campaigns revealed strong contempt for the way in which immunisation had been introduced to women at the local level. Mothers described their encounters with the authoritarian campaign-workers vividly and

emotionally. The experience was so striking that respondents in both communities marked the time in local history as the 'time of forced immunisation', *tallaalka gasab oh.*

One mother reported, 'I did not decide to take my children. I was forced during the time they were forcing people. They said, "Pay a fine, be arrested or immunise". This is the time I heard about immunisation.' Lack of adequate information, coupled with such campaign enthusiasm, incited fear and confusion about the purpose of immunisation. When recalling their experience, respondents often betrayed the tactics which had been used to avoid campaign workers, such as moving children to outlying villages or hiding them within the house. Other mothers reported about the campaign, 'There was no decision, just the Party Committee and the militia. When they come to your door, there is no decision. We are not afraid now, but in the past it was difficult. They knew every mother and they would say "She is in there, take her out".' Or again, 'During the campaigns, mothers used to be forced to take immunisation, and many mothers used to escape. This is because at the time immunisation was new and they did not know whether it would kill their children or was given for other purposes. The militia and the Party members gave mothers a very hard time. They used to check house to house for small children and take them to the immunisation place.'

Perceptions concerning the safety of immunisation

Research results indicate that the experience of the campaign strongly affected mothers' initial attitudes towards the safety of immunisation. Methods of delivery and promotion often engendered fear and prompted rumours about the severity of side-effects. As one group stated, 'After immunisation the injection site becomes sick. It does not heal very quickly, so you must return to the health service for assistance. When the mouth of the wound comes together, then something hardens on the bone and leaves a scar as if the child had been slaughtered.'

A second theme associated with safety relates to the tetanus immunisation given to women. At first, most mothers tried to refuse it, because they believed it was contraception. Rumours spread that the government was using immunisation in order to arrest population growth. Inadequate information, together with the government's drive to locate women of child-bearing age, led to suspicion of the ulterior motives behind the programme. Groups of older women expressed the strongest reservations about tetanus vaccine: 'Why vaccinate girls? It's not a good thing. It stops child-bearing. It is impossible for a girl to take this. The girls who take this vaccination are the ones who do not want to bear children and want to become prostitutes.'

Effectiveness of immunisation and perceptions of disease

Lack of awareness about immunisation, and fears about safety, raised some doubt about its effectiveness. At first, mothers reported that nothing could prevent the diseases which are brought by God: '*Ilahy iyo quranka ayaa ka horteg leh* — Only God and his Q'uran can protect us'. However, as time passed, they were able to see for themselves the benefits of immunisation. Mothers recalled that their views changed when measles appeared in the community and immunised children were not affected. The majority of women who displayed a trust in immunisation had had personal experience of its capacity to prevent disease. As one group stated, 'We have not seen an immunised child contract measles. Since immunisation began, these diseases have decreased.'

Perceptions concerning the effectiveness of immunisation also varied according to disease. It was widely thought to be effective against measles and whooping cough; but was rarely considered to offer effective protection against the other four EPI

diseases. Respondents reported marked differences in their perceptions of cause, seriousness, and children's susceptibility to each disease. For each illness, mothers described common practices for prevention and cure. Their acceptance of the measles vaccine may have been greater because they felt that measles was highly contagious and the most severe of all the EPI diseases. Moreover, respondents could not identify an exact cause for the disease, or a specific means of prevention.

On the other hand, diseases which were classified as spiritually caused, such as polio and neonatal tetanus, were hardly linked to immunisation. Unlike measles, mothers were clearly able to specify a cause for polio and neonatal tetanus. Reported methods of treatment and prevention were available from healers who specialised in these types of illness. Mothers reported that Western medical care, such as immunisation, was ineffective against spiritually related disease. Hence, traditional practices which were seen to address the cause of disease were more highly valued than vaccination.

Classification of the disease also revealed that mothers considered tetanus and neonatal tetanus to be different and distinct from each other. Tetanus was known as *tetano*, whose symptoms, cause, and treatment resembled the known medical description of tetanus. Some women had eventually accepted immunisation for prevention of tetanus in mothers. However, they did not believe the same vaccine could also prevent tetanus in newborns. Neonatal tetanus was known by a different name: *toddoba ma gaarto*, a phrase which means 'not reaching seven days'. The name refers to the fact that children with this disease usually die within a week of birth. Unlike *tetano*, its cause is spiritual, and it cannot be treated or prevented with Western medicine.

A general lack of understanding of the way in which the women and mothers perceived disease was reflected in the promotional messages used in the programme. For example, the term used to describe polio was *dabeyl*, literally 'the wind', sometimes referring to a spirit. From the respondents' perspective, *dabeyl* was a name given to a group of diseases all of which were brought by the same spirit, or *dabeyl*. Messages claiming that immunisation could prevent *dabeyl* suggested to mothers that immunisation could also prevent epilepsy, madness, and miscarriage, as well as polio. Because such messages were confusing, few mothers felt convinced of their veracity.

Health advice

Reports and observations of traditional healers illustrated their role in influencing health-seeking behaviour. By reinforcing common perceptions about disease, healers indirectly affected mothers' attitudes towards immunisation. The perceived need for immunisation against certain diseases (polio, neonatal tetanus, and tuberculosis) was often diminished by the availability of care from traditional healers. Indeed, community-based health advice proved to be a critical component of health-seeking behaviour.

A Somali proverb states that a sick man has 100 advisers, *nin buka boqol u talise*. In addition to seeking advice from doctors, pharmacies, and healers, respondents indicated that they also relied heavily on relatives and friends, especially at the early stages of illness. As one mother stated, 'Most of a mother's advice is in the neighbourhood.' The emerging trust in immunisation for measles prevention seemed to be based on the shared experience of women in the community.

Official health services

In group discussions about health advice, few mothers claimed to visit the official health service, except when encouraged during immunisation activities. Dissatisfaction with the level of care available at the MCH centre was cited by the majority of respondents as a deterrent to regular attendance: 'Immunisation is available at the MCH, but you cannot receive medicine there. There are also no skilled people to examine the children. People who have money go to the pharmacies, where they can have the medicine they need.'

Respondents conveyed the view that the MCH service rarely provided treatment when children were ill. 'There is nothing at the MCH,' stated one mother. They described services which were generally bereft both of drugs and of sympathetic health staff. Nurses were perceived as 'young, irresponsible, and careless' and often implicated in the misuse of supplies such as medicine and food. Consequently, when children fell ill, mothers preferred to seek care from reliable and trusted healers; or to purchase medicine from a pharmacy. One respondent stated: 'The government brought the food and the medicine to this MCH, but they gave it to these young girls, who always give more to someone who is a relative or a friend. Or they use it for themselves. People here are poor and have many children, so they need medicine for their sick children. The immunisation will come next.'

Mothers also complained that staff failed to explain the purpose and side-effects of immunisation. The researchers' observations confirmed these experiences. One group of mothers reported: 'The staff do not like to talk to the mothers; they do not give us much information about immunisation. In fact, they do not seem to be interested. They are doing these things just to send the mothers away.'

Discussion

Methods of promotion

Analysis of women's experience with the immunisation programme revealed that no single factor could account for low demand. Thus, it was necessary to cluster certain variables, and analyse the relationship between them and their relative influence on health-seeking behaviour. The stories told by the respondents demonstrated that many of the obstacles to adequate acceptance could be traced to programme design. From the perspective of the beneficiaries, immunisation had been introduced quickly and insensitively. Gaps in their basic understanding about the purpose of immunisation indicated that the health messages had often been misunderstood. Moreover, the way in which immunisation was promoted failed to inspire trust in its worth. Ironically, in the aftermath of the first immunisation campaigns, mothers feared for the health of their children, rather than feeling assured that they were well protected.

Throughout the global drive for UCI 90, national campaigns were often used to introduce immunisation and raise its profile. However, in Somalia, this type of social and political campaign had been employed regularly by the government to promote various other national policies. In the past, campaigns had been staged to ensure Party allegiance, improve literacy in Somali, promote self-help, and discourage tribal loyalties. Respondents likened the immunisation campaigns to these regular attempts by the government to promote its own interests. It was, therefore, not surprising that this method of promotion met with suspicion.

Throughout the duration of the programme, the responsibility for local-level mobilisation remained in the hands of the Party workers, who often had as limited a knowledge of immunisation as the mothers whom they were advising. 'Advice' about child health from the Party compared poorly with advice from trusted sources such as grandmothers, healers, and private pharmacies. Why then were so few efforts made to involve community health advisers in spreading the word about immunisation?

Context of delivery

The second most strongly reported deterrent to immunisation was the poor state of health services in Somalia. Clearly, mothers were keen to find treatment for sick children Yet few felt that the MCH could offer the quality of care which was required. Interviews with health staff confirmed this impression of the health service, citing inadequate care as the greatest obstacle to people's acceptance of immunisation. A nurse in one health clinic stated, 'The main problem in this community is that people are poor and they need treatment. We would not need to use a car with a megaphone on it to call them for immunisation if we had medicine. If we could just treat them, they would come on their own.'

The poor quality of MCH care also affected mothers' access to information about immunisation. Apart from official promotion messages, the only source of advice was the health service. Even when mothers did attend, researchers observed that health education was often poor. Many of the mothers interviewed after visiting the MCH centre could not name the vaccines their child had received, or say when they were supposed to return for subsequent doses.

When the programme began, health services throughout Somalia were generally in decline. At the time of this research, immunisation had already become the only government health service offered in many districts. Few efforts were made to improve basic health care alongside the introduction of immunisation. Available resources were generally targeted on immunisation activities alone. This approach, which focused so exclusively on immunisation delivery, appears to have contributed to low demand.

Understanding community needs

In many ways, the failure to understand needs identified at the local level hindered the success of immunisation activities in Somalia. People's perceptions of health needs and official programme objectives did not often converge. Programme managers went to great lengths to deliver immunisation. However, they placed less emphasis on demand for it. This was evident in the language used to identify different vaccine-preventable diseases. Health messages failed to reflect the widespread concepts concerning the disease; and messages consequently missed their targets.

Directly and indirectly, respondents stated that the immunisation programme seemed to exist for the benefit of those who ran it. Objectives which were inconsistent with the needs and perceptions of mothers in particular hindered the potential acceptance of immunisation.

The way in which immunisation was introduced and promoted in Somalia mimicked that of many UCI initiatives of the past decade. It was marked by enthusiasm for rapidly increasing access to a single intervention. Where the existing health infrastructure proved too weak to support the pace of expansion, it was by-passed in order to raise coverage quickly. Respondents challenged this approach by demonstrating that success was dependent not only on access to immunisation, but also on creating and sustaining a demand for it. Sustaining that demand would depend on whether programme activities were addressing the needs of beneficiaries, as well as those of programme managers and donors.

Conclusion

This research revealed an aspect of health programmes which is often neglected in planning. By reviewing individual and collective experience from the perspective of the users, managers learned for the first time how local people perceived their work. Before the collapse of the former government, the Ministry of Health and international agency personnel began to employ the research results in three ways. MCH workers and supervisors adapted health messages to reflect mothers' perceptions of immunisation and vaccine-preventable diseases. Supervisors encouraged careful attention to the language used in health education to address the most common gaps in knowledge.

Secondly, programme managers suggested that health staff should work more closely with community-based health advisers to enlist their support for immunisation promotion.

Thirdly, findings which demonstrated the importance of curative care for attracting mothers to the health service prompted the Ministry to broaden its approach to developing the sector. EPI staff requested donors and policy makers to provide resources for strengthening the MCH services as a whole, rather than concentrating all efforts exclusively on the specific intervention.

References

Ministry of Health, Expanded Programme on Immunization, 1988, '30 Cluster Survey of Immunization Coverage in Mogadishu', unpublished report.

Mohamed, A., 1986, 'Immunization Status of Two Year Old Children in Mogadiscio', unpublished PhD thesis, Somalia National University.

The author

From 1987 to 1990, Anne LaFond worked with the Expanded Programme on Immunisation in Somalia. At the time of writing she was Coordinator of the Research Programme on Sustainability in the Health Sector at Save the Children (UK). Since 1994 she has worked for the Aga Khan Foundation USA, based in Washington.

This article was first published in *Development in Practice* Volume 3, Number 1, in 1993.

Participatory appraisal in the UK urban health sector: keeping faith with perceived needs

Teresa Cresswell

Participatory Rapid Appraisal

Rapid Rural Appraisal (RRA) and its derivative Participatory Rural Appraisal (PRA) originated in developing countries as a means of evaluating the needs of poor rural communities. More recently, these methods have been adapted for use in deprived urban areas. There has been much criticism of extractive 'community research', whereby external researchers go into communities, learn from local people, leave, analyse the data, and then draw up development plans without further consultation at the community level. Rapid appraisal methods allow information about a given set of problems to be obtained quickly, without a large investment in professional time and finance. However, while these include many flexible techniques and skills suited to a community situation (such as allowing for improvisation), in practice they often fail to involve local people in each step of the process.

Participatory appraisal grew out of a concern to involve community members in research and decision-making, without losing the benefits of speed. By including local people, or those who use services, at all stages — information-gathering, analysis, action plans, and establishing priorities — the appraisal process can become empowering. A participatory approach also means that the plans are more likely to work than are those drawn up by outsiders, as they will be more firmly rooted in local conditions, be these social, financial, cultural, or political. It can also promote understanding, dialogue, and working relationships between multi-agency professionals, as well as providing greater insight into the needs of the community they serve. At best, the process can deepen people's understanding of their problems and opportunities, increase their control over development choices and plans, and initiate a process of participation that can continue as plans are put into action. This may be through community management of local initiatives, or greater awareness of the resources available to them.

In my work in the UK health sector, I currently use the term *Participatory Rapid Appraisal*, partly because I work in an urban setting; but also because 'participatory' implies that local people, as well as key outsiders, are fully involved in all stages of the process, including deciding what needs to be asked. 'Rapid' — meaning that no more than six months elapse from starting the work before concrete actions result — because this maximises people's enthusiasm and motivation, and helps them to see and participate in change, no matter how small, giving them confidence for more daunting actions. 'Appraisal' is taken to mean the whole process of deciding what needs to be asked, asking, making sense of the information, prioritising — and taking action.[1]

In using PRA to assess health needs in a deprived urban setting, we had many positive experiences. But in this article I want to discuss some of the problems encountered, so that others can learn from our insights.

Some basic principles

PRA is essentially a collection of research and communication techniques used to elicit *qualitative* data. Quantitative data can be gathered using PRA, but more traditional research methods for statistical analysis can also provide these.

Firstly, I strongly believe that *a commitment to the communities and the people who live there is a pre-requisite*. People in the UK, particularly in disadvantaged mining communities, are fed up with being used as 'research data' or for 'statistical purposes' to demonstrate the numbers of unemployed, the levels of stress, the impact on health and so on, without this making one iota of difference to them as individuals, or to their communities. In my experience, in times of recession, hardship, and bleak prospects, most people want — and actually need — something in return. It is easy for outsiders not worn down by poverty and its effects to be enthusiastic and committed to their task. Through working with people who are disadvantaged, either through poverty or ill-health, I have seen that ,unless they stand to gain something, they cannot even begin to consider the wider issues outside their immediate family and neighbourhood. This lies behind the failure of so many 'community initiatives'.[2]

So the first pre-requisite is a commitment to helping people to gain whatever 'positives' are appropriate to them as individuals wanting to improve their health.

The second is *good all-round communication skills*: you need to be able to communicate with people, not patronise them. Lobbying and advocacy also involve communicating with councils, doctors, health or social workers, or with agencies that provide financial benefits, or education. The scope is enormous.

It is important to *go at a pace that individuals are ready for*. My experience is that, while it takes a long time to engage people enough for them even to consider participating, you then have to move quickly to capitalise on their new enthusiasm and motivation. Small initiatives in response to demand give confidence, and allow people to see something working, before moving on to more difficult tasks.

It is vital to *stay with the whole process* until the community or individuals are ready and willing to take charge; researchers should then act as 'consultants' as and when required.

Finally, researchers should *avoid trying to influence the process to meet their own needs* — and be sure to have adequate resources to get started.

Learning by doing

There is often a lot of uncertainty about employing less traditional research methods, partly because of scepticism towards 'outside professionals'. But in the UK there is a growing need to find out from people themselves what it is that will improve their health. It is recognised that traditional methods of health care are not always appropriate to meet the changing needs of our communities. Statistical information will only tell us the numbers of people who are attending clinics for immunisations and so on, or the numbers of people who are suffering from a specific illness. It will not tell us why people do not make use of services available to them.

In 1988 I was hired to work part-time to identify the health needs and related social needs of an economically deprived community suffering high unemployment. The brief was to identify needs and develop services or initiatives in response to these, without the requirement of significant extra financial resources.

Staveley, a small town in north-east Derbyshire, had suffered heavy job losses when the local coal mine and chemical works closed down. The population was around 16,790. The initial task was far too great, so I broke the locality down into small distinct 'communities' or housing clusters, with which local people identified.

To select a 'community' to focus on first, I approached the relevant professionals who lived and worked in the area, and asked them which community was giving them the most concern. Health visitors, district nurses, midwives, and family doctors were asked to identify their worries, based upon health status, and attendances for recognised health checks, in particular health and development checks for babies, immunisation sessions, and ante-natal clinics. Schools were asked about attendance, and pupils' ability to take up educational opportunities. Social workers were asked about the families who were experiencing child-care difficulties, and about incidences of child abuse. The police were asked about the communities they were most concerned about, as were youth and community workers. Clergy were asked about communities and individuals who appeared to experience the greatest social difficulties. Local councillors were also asked to give their opinions and support.

It became clear that Mastin Moor, a small housing estate on the outskirts of Staveley, was thought to have the highest level of social and health problems. This mainly council-owned estate of 500 houses, with a population of about 1,800, was originally built to accommodate local miners and their families. With the pit closures, it was left with high unemployment, isolated and without easy access to health and social services, or to shops selling fresh fruit and vegetables.

Many families moved out, since it was not an ideal place to live, with no employment opportunities nearby. As a result the council had empty properties, which were used by people who were homeless or in need. This quickly destroyed any 'community' spirit and comradeship, and a divided community evolved, with poor social networks and family-support systems.

I set out to find what the families who lived in Mastin Moor perceived their main health and social problems to be. I did this quite subjectively. I knocked on the doors of households which looked as though they were not coping: for example, homes which seemed neglected, whose gardens were litter-strewn, or full of junk. Or I stopped mothers in the street, at the school gates, or in a local playgroup. I asked health visitors to identify families that might be willing to talk to me.

I used informal open-ended questions about what they thought their health and social problems were, and recorded information in a small notebook. The main themes were of social isolation, limited access to health and social care, the lack of pre-school provision, and the lack of anywhere to meet. This reinforced the views of the local professionals, and confirmed my own observations.

I did no further investigation and decided to develop a social project in response to these specific needs. With the support of nine mothers, we met several times in their homes to discuss the way forward. They identified an under-used community centre to set up a 'drop-in' service, with creche facilities. It was to be a place for mothers and others to meet and socialise, and develop other initiatives they thought would be useful. The project was well supported by the local health visitor, who was regularly available.

The most important aspect was that the mothers had full control over the project. They ran it, and we were there only by invitation. It went on to include the provision of sewing machines and classes in sewing, joinery, and photography; health-education sessions on relationships, human sexuality, child care, cot deaths; and much more. They ran jumble sales to raise money and organised outings for the children. The project grew from nine mothers in October to over 100 members (not including the children!) the following June. Over 20 women went with their children to a residential college, for training in assertiveness and other skills. Several went on to further education, and others to paid jobs.

This experience taught me the importance of handing over to local people, not making decisions on their behalf but developing a process whereby they can acquire the confidence to take more control over their lives. Through this, they become more articulate in identifying their real needs: and, more importantly, they take better advantage of what resources are available.[3]

Naming the process

I had no name for this methodology, but the process was simple: ask the people who live there, and the people who provide the services, and look for yourself. Match the three with any existing statistical data, and you can begin to identify the main needs. Then allow community members to decide how they want to tackle the problem. This should ensure community ownership and participation, and start the process of empowering people.

I later attended a lecture given by Professor Hugh Annette of the Liverpool School of Tropical Medicine (LSTM), a pioneer in the use of PRA in Health Care in Urban Settings in the UK. We met and talked about incorporating some of these techniques in my work. North Derbyshire Health Authority is quite innovative, and was already using less traditional techniques to reach local people, and develop services more appropriate to what they perceived their needs to be. So the Authority was very receptive to my using PRA techniques.

The Danesmoor Project

The formal use of PRA in north Derbyshire was set up in Danesmoor, a community of about 3,000, not unlike Mastin Moor. When the estate was built in the 1950s, houses were allocated to Coal Board employees in order of status: at that time people viewed it with pride. With the recession and pit closures of the 1970s and 1980s, the community suffered severe unemployment, which accounted for over 15 per cent of the population by late 1991. In the 1970s, a new housing policy meant that accommodation on the estate was based not on employment but on need. People rehoused there did not necessarily share the traditional working-class values of others already on the estate. As outsiders moved in, there was no work or social focus to offset the destruction of the old community; about 60 per cent of households relied on Housing Benefit (a form of public assistance). The community is sharply divided: those who are in paid employment, the original mining community, and the elderly form one group; while unemployed people and single-parent families form the other. The latter were identified as experiencing more problems with children and with vandalism.

The initial aim was to identify the health and social needs of the various population groups in the community, such as elderly or middle-aged people, families, children, and so on. We based our approach on the experience of Hugh Annette and Susan Rifkin in Sefton (Liverpool), and their book *WHO Guidelines for Rapid Appraisal to Assess Community Needs: A Focus on Health Improvements for Low Income Areas* (1980).

It was felt that the only way in which statutory agencies can be truly participative is for the 'management' (that is people who have direct access to financial and other resources) to leave their offices, get to know the communities, and ask the questions. Three managers would do each interview — two asking questions, and one taking notes — to reduce the element of bias. The idea was that these would belong to a multi-sectoral team, but this proved impossible to achieve, not because they were unwilling; but because it proved unrealistic to get three managers from different agencies to meet up, be trained in PRA techniques and interviewing skills, spend time on interviewing and then more time on the analysis — although we did give it a try. More significantly, we decided that the participation of statutory authorities (Health Service, Education, Social Services) should be their *commitment to allocate resources to outcomes of the research.*

A Steering Group was set up to oversee the project, with a health visitor, a family doctor, a social worker, a school nurse, and others from the social services, community education, and local health authority. They were all new to PRA, and not enough time was given to helping them to understand the process, its strengths and limitations. This led to confusion about what the exercise could achieve. There were difficulties in deciding 'what questions to ask', and how to respond to the findings. Our main mistake was trying to move too quickly, without a working understanding of what we could achieve.

The step-by-step process[4]

1 A Steering Group was established to oversee the project and design questions, based upon the data we already had and professional concerns for the area.

2 Questions focused on four broad themes:

- People's perceptions of the area and the community: what is it like living there?
- The evident health and social problems.
- Existing care-service provision, and community needs.
- Within reason, what would benefit individuals, families, and the community as a whole?

3 Health visitors, school nurses, and district nurses were all 'advised' that this was going to 'happen' to them, which unfortunately created a feeling of antagonism towards the PRA process and its outcomes. And they were all so busy that there was little opportunity to participate. However, health visitors contacted certain families to facilitate our talking to people in the area.

4 It was impossible to get other professionals to help in the interviewing process.

Community members were approached, and after several weeks five mothers said they would like to train. Creche provision was made. But they did not follow through, for various reasons: a job offer, moving home, feeling too scared, no time.

All I could do was proceed on my own. Several weeks into asking questions, one 'key community member' said she would like to help. She was a local councillor, a single parent already working for a social-work certificate, and had lived in the community all her life. She was a real asset.

5 Over 54 interviews — not including sessions with 200 children in eight school groups — were completed over a three-month period, though only about 34 working days were actually spent on this part of the exercise. I was involved in all of these, except where I had worked with people previously, since this might have hindered free communication. The interviews were with three main groups:

a. Key Professionals
Health Visitors
District Nurses
School Nurses
Family Doctors
Head Teachers
Nursery Teacher
Librarian
Midwife
Community Mental Health Workers
Social Workers
Domiciliary Services Organiser
Police Inspector
Housing Manager
Clergy
Pharmacist
Dentist
Youth Leader

b. Key Community Members
Councillors
Shopkeeper
Publican
Welfare Rights Worker
Playgroup Leader
Five Key Community Members

c. Community Members
23, including 10 lone parents
200+ children

6 Interviews took place in people's own homes or place of work. They were confidential, and took about one hour each. Interviewees were advised that interviews would be documented, and that I would read back my notes to them, or they could read them for themselves. This gave people confidence that what I had written was what they had said. It also enabled clarification, and served as a memory-jogger to elicit further information.

The one-hour limit was to respect their busy lives, and the fact that after this time people tend to become repetitive, and get tired. In fact, only about 30 minutes was given to pure 'fact finding'. Fifteen minutes were for selling the project, and 15 more for clarification and closing the interview.

All the interviews were recorded in one shorthand notebook. Analysis and further writing took about 25 working days after the interviews had been completed.

7 I recorded one focus-group discussion on video, and we photographed relevant features in the area: a litter-strewn river, and an inadequate bridge. The quality and type of houses were photographed, as were play areas and so on. This made it easier to relay information back to the authorities.

8 It soon emerged that the main difficulties on this estate concerned single parents, and their relations with established members of the community. For this reason the project — which was supposed to be generic — changed to focus only on the needs of such parents. This is the beauty of PRA. It is flexible, and this change did not compromise our project. It was acknowledged that the needs of other community members would have to be investigated to get the full picture.

9 A number of priority needs were identified and mutually agreed by the participants:
- a central facility for community and social activities;
- relocation of professionals as a multi-disciplinary team within the community;
- a nursery and pre-school activities;
- the inclusion of community activities within the school;
- facilities and resources for young people;
- improved parks and play areas;
- an investigation into the dangers of toxic waste from a local factory, and other environmental issues;
- a community newsletter and better communication systems.

10 Feedback was a problem. I was under pressure to complete the work and present it to the Health Authority. An interim report was produced for discussion, and an open meeting was held, to which all participants were individually invited. It was attended by about 30 people. Members of the Health Authority were unhappy with the outcomes, and with people's perception of their services; and unfortunately they took the report to be final, rather than the basis for what could have been a productive dialogue. Community members were very happy with the report: one said, 'It's the best thing that has come out of Danesmoor'.

It also caused a lot of bad feeling between health professionals and myself. They felt that the sample gave a biased perception of the services, and was too small to be of consequence. They tried to dismiss community members' 'needs' as 'wants'. Some workers felt that it was not appropriate for them to attend an open meeting; and to my knowledge they never responded to the report. Comments such as 'We knew all that anyway' were typical. In reality, I suspect they were hurt by the negative feedback on the services, and tried to dismiss the criticism as unrepresentative and personal. Whatever the reasons, it affected their ability to consider the changing needs of the community they served.

11 There were many organisational problems. At a management level, there was not enough commitment to considering how to change service-delivery to meet current 'consumer' needs. The project was inadequately resourced, and there was no one in post to follow up the study (though this has since been resolved, with a community health post designated for the area).

Many professionals, especially in the health service, did not understand the PRA process, or have confidence in qualitative research, and so they tried to discredit it by focusing on quantitative aspects of the study. Nevertheless, the doctors were well aware of the harmful effects that social and economic disadvantage can have on health.

Community members complained about the lack of resources and help in meeting the priorities identified.

On the positive side, some agencies as well as the local council did take up the findings of the study; a Danesmoor Action Group developed; and single mothers were enabled to get together and form new friendships and support networks.[5]

Some lessons for the future

What we learned from this experience is that before undertaking any such exercise it is vital to take the time to involve all the relevant professionals and community members, ensuring that they understand the process, and what the outcomes may be. We also realised that, although PRA is quicker and more flexible than traditional methods, it needs to be complemented by other research data.

The overall aim was to provide a means for professionals and local people to unite in order to improve the health of the community. Incorporating PRA should enable service-providers to understand the 'whys' and possible 'hows' when it comes to making changes to existing provision. It can help professionals to be more responsive to people's own perceptions of need, and creates new potential for dialogue between the providers and users of services. By breaking down barriers, it can promote an atmosphere of partnership which is important not only in the initial stages of any project, but also for evaluation. *But attracting people to participate is the hardest part of the exercise.*

Following this, we set up a project in which local people were paid to train as interviewers, so we could get a 'complete community perspective'. This is not easy, since most people feel they have nothing to contribute, and that they are not 'good enough' to be interviewers. However, experience shows that, once they are trained and fully involved in the process, people enjoy it and gain confidence. But because of some reticence to accept the Danesmoor findings, we involved more interviewers, who went back for two or three follow-up sessions to check the validity of the findings. We work on the premise that in the first interview people tell us what they think we want to know. In the second, they tell us what they know. In the third, they tell it how it really is.

An example of this approach is the Safe Communities Project, in which we aimed to identify the safety needs of a community that had experienced a relatively high rate of childhood accidents. While it was not always easy to use the information gathered from local people, the practical outcomes were successful. We set up first aid and home-safety courses, while the police installed safety cameras, and local schools became involved in a major safety campaign. We later received funding for a low-cost home-safety equipment scheme, with a local store acting as the retail outlet. This avoided the stigma attached to 'hand-outs', and allowed people freedom of choice in deciding what, if any, equipment to instal.

Once health and other authorities accept that qualitative research using PRA can help them to understand people's needs, it is imperative to back this up quickly with action, so that changes can be evaluated. What is important is not the size of the project, but the fact that it works, that it involves people at all decision-making levels, and that the outcomes, no matter how small, can be seen.

The results of the action may take time. For example, the Poolsbrook and Duckmanton Health Projects began in 1993, in communities disadvantaged through loss of jobs, river pollution, isolation, and high public-transport costs. The concept was to provide £10,000 per year to each community for three years for the purposes of improving their health and social needs. The process was protracted. People were at first uncertain about taking responsibility for the money: 'What if we get it wrong?' It was sometimes hard to convince them that there were no rights or wrongs, only outcomes. Once they took on the responsibility, they came up with more ideas than they had money to spend, including many that would not have been thought of by health workers or other professionals. For example, when the coal mines were working, the community were screened for chest complaints. Now they are shut, people continue to live in an area that is mined by open-cast methods, so they still experience dust-related problems; but there is no mass screening. Could the money be spent on that? The dialogue has been rich. The communities are now making very good decisions. Being given responsibility has enabled them to consider their options seriously, putting them on a stronger footing in dialogue with the service-providers. It has been a learning experience for everyone, and one of the most important outcomes has been the development of mutual respect.

I work on the counselling concept that 'enough is enough'. In other words, if it is good enough for the clients, leave it. If they can work with what they have, know, and understand, don't complicate it. People will come back when they are ready. The strength of PRA is that it accepts diversity, by 'triangulating' or using several sources and means of gathering information, and perspectives. 'Truth' is approached through building up diverse data — direct observation, semi-structured interviews, putting together diagrams, using photographs and video — to contribute to a progressively more accurate analysis of the situation.

Dialogue is essential, to avoid the problems that arise when local people's concerns are perceived as criticism of local professionals. Community members and professionals must be involved throughout the process. Data and findings should be recorded accurately, checked, and fed back quickly. This maintains information-exchange, and enables us to capitalise on people's enthusiasm and motivation. Otherwise the key feature of 'speed' is lost. Attempting something small, that is achievable, gives vital confidence — to the funders, the professionals, and, most importantly, to the community as a whole.

No external professionals could adequately express the feelings behind statements made in the interviews, such as 'We need help, not blame', or 'People think I don't care, rather than can't manage'. This is evident when outsiders interpret 'needs' as 'wants', thus diminishing people's own perceptions of the situation in which they live. People coping with poverty and hardship place a different emphasis on many aspects of life, some of which may seem insignificant to an outsider, but they enhance or degrade the daily life of the individuals concerned. Those who play a professional role cannot reliably interpret the 'needs' of community members, nor make effective decisions for those communities, without first understanding how these needs are seen by people themselves.

If professionals are to be more responsive to individuals and communities, we have a duty to respect their perceptions and perceived needs and to use the information constructively to enter into a dialogue which will enable us to develop truly responsive community-based initiatives.

Notes

1 The term 'rapid' is questioned by many, who feel the emphasis should be less on speed and more on acquiring 'usable quality information'. A preferable title might be Participatory Appraisal, with the understanding that it is rapid.

2 I do not believe that people in Western urban settings have a concept of 'community', nor that they are necessarily altruistic. When people struggle with

adversity, they have little left to give. The old saying 'When poverty comes through the door, love flies out of the window' sums this up well. People have problems in meeting their own needs, and often feel as though they are getting nothing back for themselves. This is why the concept of community does not function as well as we might want. If we embark on any kind of PRA, there should be built into it a method of 'giving back' to individuals, to improve social and health opportunities, and build self-esteem. Only when people feel they are getting something in return will they feel like contributing to 'community' actions — and even then we may in fact be talking about neighbourliness or shared interests (such as being parents of children at the same school) rather than a broader commitment to 'community'.

3 A more detailed account of this project can be found in my report for the North Derbyshire Health Authority, 'PRA — An Investigation Into the Health and Social Needs of People Living in Danesmoor — In Particular the Needs of Single Parents and Children' (1992).

4 This and a similar project was filmed by WHO in a video entitled 'The District', which compared 'bottom-up' approaches to health care in three countries: Zimbabwe, Indonesia, and the UK.

5 A sample of the practical steps that have been taken following the PRA exercise and report includes starting up a mother and toddler group; getting the police to provide two special constables to patrol the area (which succeeded in halving petty crimes and teenage vandalism); getting the council to agree a special fund for any community group willing to assist in an environmental clean-up; looking into the possibility of formal and informal play areas; introducing a dog warden service to address the problem of fouling in public areas; removing public obstructions from pavements, to allow access for wheelchairs and pushchairs and reduce safety hazards; investigating concerns about pollution and toxic waste; and making a formal application from the Danesmoor Community Group for a community house.

The author

Teresa Cresswell holds a joint post of Locality Health Promotion Coordinator with the North Derbyshire Health Authority and Primary Care Development Co-ordinator with the Community Health Care Service (North Derbyshire) Trust. She is a registered nurse and health visitor, and currently Manager, in coordination with the Chester-field Employment Services Agency, of the Unemployment and Health Project.

This article was first published in *Development in Practice*, Volume 6, Number 1, in 1996.

Stressed, depressed, or bewitched?
A perspective on mental health, culture, and religion

Vikram Patel, Jane Mutambirwa, and Sekai Nhiwatiwa

Introduction

Mental illness, in its broadest sense, is one of the commonest afflictions affecting the human race. The World Bank report on health and development (1993), though criticised for the unreliability of some of its data, identified 'neuropsychiatric' disease as the second-most important non-communicable cause of disability in the developing world (Blue and Harpham, 1994). Of these diseases, depression was the single most important diagnosis. The report emphasises an aspect of health which is intimately related to a community's overall health status and development, and which has been ignored by development agencies and Health Ministries faced with the pressing claims of communicable diseases and the health problems of mothers and children. However, it is impossible to separate the mental and spiritual components of health from physical illness, in particular when dealing with chronic illness and maternal and child health problems. It is likely, and desirable, that future health-related development work will, and should, include mental health among its priorities. With this future in mind, we focus in this article on the close relationship between mental health, culture, and religion. We hope to inform those who are involved in mental-health services in sub-Saharan Africa (SSA) of the problems caused by simply translating concepts and ideas developed in the very different societies of Western Europe and North America (referred to as 'Euro-American' in this article), whence the bulk of development funds originate. Instead, we will attempt to show that community health problems and service delivery must involve understanding and assisting those with mental-health problems from within the context of their own society. Although we focus on SSA nations, because of our personal experiences in Zimbabwe, we believe that much of what applies to these settings may apply to other less developed countries also.

The article begins with a description of what is meant by the term 'mental illness' and moves on to examining some of the ways in which culture and religion influence mental illness. We end with our views on how culturally appropriate mental-health services should be developed.

What is mental illness?

It is of great importance for all health and development workers to recognise that the term 'mental illness' does not refer to a homogeneous group of problems, but rather to a number of different types of disorder. It is even more important to recognise that, although every society has people it views as mentally ill, the use and construction of this concept may vary considerably from one society to another. The group of disorders most often associated with mental illness are the psychotic and affective disorders, such as schizophrenia and mania. There is little doubt that such severe disturbances, which affect virtually all aspects of a person's mental and behavioural life, are recognised in most cultures and societies in SSA (Patel, 1995). It is this group of disorders which occupies so much of the time and financial resources of mental-health services in Euro-American societies and for which psychiatric drug treatments have proven to be of considerable value. Despite the powerful evidence of a genetic role in the aetiology of these disorders, the environment plays at least as great a role in determining the course and outcome. For instance, schizophrenia seems to have a better outcome in developing countries, despite the fact that mental-health services are underdeveloped in these very settings. In other words, even though Europe and North America have extensive mental-health and social-welfare services, people with schizophrenia fare worse in those countries than sufferers in India or Nigeria. Recognising that the course of even the most 'medical' of all mental illnesses is so profoundly influenced by socio-environmental factors gives cause for concern to those who wish to recreate a mental-health service modelled on the Euro-American system of health care, without evaluating the possible therapeutic ingredients already existing in some SSA societies, such as the role of the extended family and traditional treatments.

Another group of disorders classified by Euro-American psychiatry as mental illnesses has been historically called the neuroses. These disorders may be thought of as exaggerated forms of normal reactions to stressful events. Thus, anxiety, depression, and physical symptoms in the absence of a physical disease are experienced by many people in response to stressful events, and in neuroses these experiences become more intense and often out of proportion to the stressors (Gelder *et al.*, 1983). Over time, such problems have been conceptualised as

mental illnesses, not least because of the Cartesian dichotomy which for over a century has influenced thinking in the field of bio-medicine (by which we mean modern Western medicine, based on the principles of the natural sciences). This dichotomy holds that the body and mind are distinct. Although contemporary health practitioners are encouraged to consider the integrated role of both mind and body in their patients, if patients present with symptoms for which there are no corresponding physical signs or findings, many practitioners will conclude that they must be mentally ill. As psychiatry and its allied professions have evolved in the North, such vague and poorly defined illness entities have become reified into precise categories; the latest WHO classification of mental disorders includes no fewer than 60 categories of illnesses previously classified as neuroses, including phobias, anxiety disorders, and mild depressions (WHO, 1992). Neurotic disorders are the commonest group of mental illnesses and are particularly common in primary care and community settings; recent studies in Zimbabwe suggest that up to a quarter of clinic attenders may be distressed. In this article, we refer to this group of problems as *psychosocial distress* because, as we will discuss later, referring to them as a mental illness is fraught with conceptual problems.

There are several other areas of health problems in which psychiatry has claimed an expertise, including childhood problems such as conduct disorders, abuse, and mental handicap; the abuse of substances such as alcohol and drugs; mental disorders associated with HIV infection; and the psychological consequences of violence and trauma. While each type of disorder has its own unique characteristics, there are some common features such as, for example, the influence of adverse socio-economic events on these disorders as well. Thus, many of the general points made in this article would apply to these disorders.

Religion, culture, and mental illness

These are complex issues which have been of great interest to anthropologists, and more recently to mental health professionals. Within the scope of this article, we will focus on some areas to illustrate how religious and cultural factors are intimately related to mental illness in the community. While we recognise that culture and religion are complex and dynamic concepts, in focusing on the relationship between mental illness and culture and religion in this article, we have taken a unitary, and perhaps simplistic, view of these concepts.

Concepts of mental illness

The medical speciality of psychiatry has its roots in Euro-American professional views of mental illness. This is vividly demonstrated by WHO classifications of mental illness, which, though purporting to be 'international', dismiss illness types described in non-Euro-American cultures as either 'culture-bound' or not even worthy of recognition (Patel and Winston, 1994). The commonest neurotic disorders, in this classification, are depression and anxiety. Patients in Euro-American societies increasingly understand that concepts such as 'depression' relate to a state of psychological distress. Over time, the health worker and patient acquire similar explanatory models for the distress state. In many SSA societies such disorders are recognised as being distress states, but are not understood in the same way: the concepts used to understand and explain their causes and nature may differ widely. Thus, similar states of distress evoke recognition from the local community and health workers in Harare, but the causes are perceived as closely linked to the interaction of social, economic, and spiritual problems (see below) afflicting the person (Patel *et al.*, 1995). The same concept, *semantically* translated, can be elicited in this and other

societies, but may *mean* something quite different; for example, rather than being viewed as a mental problem, it may reflect the patients' assessment of their socio-economic and spiritual state.

The difficulties in translating even basic concepts are illustrated by our experience with an apparently simple question, asking patients about any previous history of emotional or mental illness. In Euro-American societies, a substantial proportion of people would understand this to include depression, anxiety, or indeed many stressful situations which resulted in their consulting a health worker. It was virtually impossible to translate the question adequately into the Shona language, without giving the impression that we were dealing either with 'madness' (and thus alienating most of our patients) or 'stress' (which many of them experience, owing to adverse socio-economic circumstances). This is a seemingly trivial example, but it represents the very heart of the issue of mental health and development. It is for this reason that we refer to neurotic mental disorders as *psycho-social distress states*.

In many societies, then, such distress states are not viewed from a medical standpoint. If depression is not considered to be a 'mental illness' (as psychiatry understands it), then should we attempt to change the entire meaning of the term, so that it conforms to the dominant Euro-American paradigm? Is there any evidence to suggest that the 'medicalising' of such distress states, as opposed to the application of socio-spiritual models, has produced any significant benefit to patients? While recognising that the fundamental experience of a distress state is universal to all humans, we believe that the contextual meaning of the distress is of singular importance. Such meanings should be respected and understood, rather than referring to an imposed foreign model to explain the problem.

One area which illustrates the complex interaction of personal misfortune, religious beliefs, and cultural values is that of witchcraft. Although witchcraft is outlawed in many African societies, beliefs in its power remain alive, and sociologists have argued that such belief systems help to make misfortune understandable (Chavunduka, 1994). From a Euro-American perspective, what does feeling bewitched mean? Can it be reduced to a psychiatric 'symptom'? Or is this belief a way that some communities have developed to explain why life has its difficult moments? Should the diverse and unproven psycho-theories of the North, like psycho-analysis and general systems theory, be imposed on other cultures?

Idioms of psycho-social distress

Beyond these broad concepts is the issue of idioms used by people in psycho-social distress. A fundamental difference between mental health and physical health is that, in assessing mental health, one relies almost entirely on what a person tells the health worker. Language becomes the very essence of expressing distress, and emotional terms such as 'sadness' and 'fear' cannot be translated without examining the overall context of the use of these terms in a community (Lutz, 1985).

Idioms like 'feeling sad' have gradually become professionalised by medical personnel into 'symptoms' and then taken one step further into becoming 'criteria' for specific types of 'mental illness'. This process is intimately related to the historical evolution of conceptualising human distress in Euro-American culture. However, much mental-health research and development in SSA societies has assumed that the idioms of mental-health problems as defined in Euro-American settings can be applied simply by a semantic translation of terms. The following examples show how this approach may confound the process of interpreting the manifestations of psycho-social distress in different cultures.

The idiom of 'hopelessness' is central to the Euro-American model of depression, and questions such as 'Do you have hope for the future?' are often asked of the patient. However, in the context of Buddhist cultures in Sri Lanka, Obeysekere argues that a negative answer to this question indicates not 'a depressive, but a good Buddhist'. Thus, 'hopelessness lies in the nature of the world, and salvation lies in understanding and overcoming that hopelessness' (Obeysekere, 1985). In this context, then, eliciting the idiom of hopelessness would yield positive responses, but the contextual meaning of the term is very different. In the Shona language, the term for sadness is *kusuwa*. This term not only implies personal sorrow and grief, but is also used in the context of describing an emotional state which is a prerequisite for sympathy, empathy, and reaching out for help and is, in this context, a positive emotion.

Another example is the spiritual experiential events which occur in many religious movements in African societies. Thus, hearing or feeling the Holy Spirit, feeling that the ancestral spirits wish to come out or express themselves, or sensations of being possessed by such spirits are not only commonplace among members of some religious groups, but indeed are highly valued personal experiences. If mental-health workers are unaware of the contexts of these experiences, they may see them as symptoms of a mental illness.

Priests, prophets, and psychiatrists: what do people do when in distress?

In Zimbabwe, religion is inseparable from health, and this relationship applies to both traditional and Christian religions. First, let us consider the relationship of traditional medicine and religion. Traditional medical practices of the indigenous people have a religious foundation, based on local views on the creation of humankind, the life cycle, concepts of growth and development, and the purpose of life in the Creator's scheme of things. In Zimbabwe, and many other sub-Saharan African societies, there are extensive beliefs in a spiritual world inhabited by ancestral, alien, clan, and evil spirits. These beliefs play an important role in guiding people when they are distressed (Mutambirwa, 1989). Traditional healers are recognised by many as being able to heal the sick, by virtue of their intimate knowledge of herbal medicines and their special ability to be possessed by or communicate with spirits. When seen in a Euro-American context, traditional healers assume many roles, including those of a priest, a legal adviser, a social worker, and a counsellor (Staugard, 1985).

Christianity is the most popular denomination of organised religion in Zimbabwe. The origins of Christianity are historically linked with the colonisation of this region. Christian missionaries believed that traditional religion was pagan. Since beliefs in spiritual causation were inextricably interwoven with misfortune and illness, traditional medicine was also unacceptable. The repression of traditional beliefs by missionaries, in collusion with the colonial administration, led to large numbers of people taking up the Christian faith and being taught to shun traditional healers. Many Zimbabweans today claim Christianity as their main religion, but in practice many such Christians continue to believe in the power of witchcraft and of their ancestral spirits and see little conflict between these beliefs and official Church doctrine (Bourdillon, 1987). Furthermore, Christianity is practised in this region in diverse ways, with a wide range of 'independent', Pentecostal, and Evangelical churches, some of which syncretise Christianity and indigenous religious beliefs. It is not uncommon to see charismatic pastors, in particular from the Apostolic churches, who assume the role of a spiritual healer and heal the sick with the power of the Holy Spirit, make prophecies for the future, and encourage the congregation to join in spiritual experiences, including trance states and speaking in incomprehensible 'tongues'. Interestingly, some Apostolic churches shun both

'scientific' and traditional medicine, relying instead on the Prophets and faith-healers within their church for healing.

The dichotomy between 'scientific' and traditional medicine is rooted in the frequently held belief that bio-medicine is superior when applied to physical and bodily aspects of health, by virtue of prescriptions of scientifically prepared medicines, operative procedures, investigations, and hospitalisations. On the other hand, traditional healing and faith-healing are often viewed as providing a holistic health-care service. Thus, health problems associated with the physical body as well as with the mind-soul and the social and spiritual environments are healed (Chavunduka, 1978). While psycho-social distress states have become medical-ised and in Euro-American society are increasingly treated by a growing legion of mental-health workers ranging from counsellors to psychiatrists, in Zimbabwe and many other SSA societies these distress states are often inextricably linked to spiritual and social factors. In keeping with these beliefs, a significant number of people suffering from psycho-social problems consult religious leaders such as pastors, priests, prophets, and traditional healers in search of emotional relief.

Helping people with psycho-social problems

In Euro-American society, theories to explain personal distress have moved from the spiritual realms to the psycho-analytical realms and, more recently, to a host of new theories including cognitive, behavioural, systemic, social, and interpersonal theories. Each of these conceptualises distress states or illness categories according to certain theoretical postulates, which are then extended to actual therapeutic interventions to alleviate the distress. Success with such a therapy is then used as a validator of the theory itself. One example of such a therapy which has gained prominence in Euro-American society is cognitive therapy, in particular for depressive states. Like many contemporary approaches, it emphasises the personal responsibility of the patient in attaining the cure. Cognitive theory postulates that the fundamental problem in conditions which manifest as depression or anxiety is maladaptive thinking. The treatment is aimed at assisting the individual to recognise the maladaptive nature of his or her thinking and then attempt to change this. This theory is firmly rooted in the introspective individualism of the North, and is in sharp contrast to the 'external' models of distress in communities in SSA. To date, we are not aware of any studies attempting to evaluate the effectiveness of these psycho-therapeutic models in SSA. Furthermore, it is well recognised that one of the most powerful predictors of response to psycho-therapy is the 'congruence' or sharing of models of illness by therapist and patient, so that those patients who are 'psychologically minded' are the ones most likely to respond. We would argue that the same principle may be applied to other cultures, so that therapies whose theoretical models are congruent for patients and healers are likely to be successful: spiritual rituals, for example, are likely to be effective for spiritual problems. This, of course, would be at odds with trying to change the patient's view of the problem so as to suit an alternative, often imported model used by the therapist.

One example from Shona culture is the behavioural state of *kutanda botso*. This state, which is characterised by a person wandering away from home dressed in rags and begging, may be seen to be similar to the psychiatric category of 'brief reactive psychosis'. However, it is often a traditionally sanctioned ritual to cleanse a person who has committed a grievous social crime such as striking his or her parents. By adopting such a vagrant role, perpetrators will absolve their misdeeds and correct the spiritual imbalance caused by their actions. Is family therapy, as prescribed by Euro-American practitioners, superior to this form of traditional treatment? Or is the increasing use of 'therapy' as a judicial recommendation for people who break social codes and laws, such as sexual offenders in the North, in fact an analogy to Shona sanctions?

Many imported models employ techniques which are not culturally acceptable to patients in other societies. For example, many patients expect to be told what to do to alleviate their distress, and the role of the silent facilitator, typical of some Euro-American psycho-therapies, may be inappropriate in many counselling situations. This is clearly evoked by the 'guru–chela' relationship between counsellor and patient described in India, in which the psycho-therapeutic relationship mimics that between a teacher and student, with emphasis on the counsellor providing direct advice and guidance to the patient. Indeed, dependence on others in the Indian context is a desirable state of existence and does not have the negative connotation which it carries in Euro-American society (Saxena, 1994).

Developing appropriate mental-health services

We have demonstrated some of the ways in which culture and religion are profoundly intertwined with mental health and illness. In this section, we consider how mental-health services may be developed in a manner which is culturally appropriate.

Most development activity in mental health imitates Euro-American models of illness and health-care delivery. These ignore the contextual meaning of such culturally defined terms and categories of illness and the role played by 'non-professionals' in the alleviation of distress. When seeking to fund or provide new services, agencies concentrate their efforts on creating new positions of counsellors and on training them in methods of counselling developed in altogether different settings. All too often, this is done without examining what was already happening in the particular setting, as if people with psycho-social problems were previously unattended to. Development activity catering to vulnerable groups of individuals, such as refugees or HIV-infected people, identifies counselling as one of the ways of alleviating their distress. However, it remains unclear whether this has involved working with the pre-existing network of 'informal' counsellors. In Zimbabwe, it appears that some of the counselling approaches mimic imported methods, such as systematic therapy, and employ counsellors with a professional background modelled on Euro-American health-care approaches. Only rarely does one encounter any published, structured evaluation of the impact of these counselling techniques on the life of the patient. It seems that this issue is often taken for granted, under the assumption that if it works in Euro-American society, then it must do so in other societies.

In this context, we wish to point out that 'cultural spectacles' affect not only Euro-American workers but also growing numbers of people in SSA, who, by virtue of education and/or religion modelled on Euro-American societies, are equally in conflict with the majority of their kin. For example, professional 'scientific' medicine has taken firm root throughout the world, and its practitioners in Zimbabwe, though themselves coming from a society with rich and extensive beliefs in ancestral spirits, will often suppress these traditional beliefs because of the dismissive attitude taken by what is historically a Euro-American discipline of health care. Such health workers, though integrated within the bio-medical approach to health delivery, are not necessarily representative spokespeople for the community at large. A very recent example of this is an epidemic of measles which led to the deaths of several children from a particular Apostolic church whose congregation shun bio-medical treatment and immunisation. Most policy makers and health workers in the medical services were appalled by this apparent neglect by the parents, but they were oblivious to the power of religion and culture in influencing treatment choices in Zimbabwe.

The close bonds between religion, culture, and mental health in many societies in SSA have important lessons for development and health workers involved in mental-health care. In attempting to provide mental-health services, including counselling, to any population, development funds should be targeted at what the culture finds acceptable and workable, rather than trying to recreate a Northern model. The first step must be to get a close understanding of the religious beliefs and social structure of the society and to investigate the pre-existing network of informal counsellors. Research into the nature and cause of psycho-social distress is an essential prerequisite to delivering services. Collaboration with local health workers from professional backgrounds akin to those of their Euro-American colleagues must be extended to local priests, traditional healers, village chiefs, and community workers selected by the community. For any mental-health initiative to be successful, it must reach out to the ordinary person and must be sensitive to his or her world-view. And most important, one must refrain from imposing an invalid foreign category, since this will only alienate the people it is meant to help. We need to understand what the community means by mental health and illness, its priorities in mental-health care, what it believes are the ways in which such problems can be tackled, and so on. Idioms of distress need to be generated from the language of the people, rather than relying on simple translations from a foreign language. There is little doubt that many themes of distress are universal to humanity, but it is equally important to recognise those characteristics of distress unique to a particular community. Any intervention must be evaluated from the context of the individual and the health-care worker. New measures, such as the Shona version of the WHO Quality of Life Instrument (Kuyken *et al.*, 1994) and the Shona Symptom Questionnaire (Patel *et al.*, 1994) may be used to evaluate counselling and other interventions for psycho-social distress.

The influence of religion and culture on mental health is being recognised in Euro-American society, where increasing numbers of professionals are writing about the need to recognise the spiritual dimension of a person's health (Cox, 1994; Sims, 1994). We would go further in stating that this dimension is important not just for mental health, but for physical illness as well, in particular for severe illnesses such as AIDS, for which medical treatments remain unaffordable, unavailable, or ineffective. These spiritual dimensions are rarely accessible to bio-medically trained health workers, who should admit this and allow open access to such patients by religious and traditional healers. This already hapens in facilities for terminally ill and psychiatric patients in Europe and North America (Stephens, 1994). Ironically, in societies where spirituality and health are inextricably linked, health workers seem to resist this need of their patients.

Conclusions

Mental illness is a significant cause of disability in the development world and has been largely ignored in health-related development activity. In many SSA societies, the impact of economic structural adjustment in impoverishing the people, the breakdown of traditional community and family relationships caused by urban migration, and the devastating effect of AIDS are likely to cause an even greater impact on the psycho-social health of individuals. There is abundant evidence that most of these problems are not adequately dealt with in government-funded primary health-care settings. In such a situation, our most urgent message is that mental health needs to be firmly on the agenda of development activity. It is important to recognise that mental illness as defined in Euro-American society does not translate with the same contextual meaning in many African countries. Thus, what is often regarded as a mental illness is to be found in the broader realms of socio-spiritual problems, which we prefer to call psycho-social distress. Such distress is intimately related to a community's overall sense of well-being and development, to its economic strength, to its network of social and spiritual relationships, and to the indigenous health carers and religious leaders in that community. In delivering mental-health services, development activity should recognise these important interactions between mental health, culture, and religion.

Acknowledgements

We thank Mark and Cathy Winston, Paul Linde, and Laurie Schultz for their comments on this paper. Vikram Patel is supported by the Beit Medical Fellowships, GTZ (Harare) and IDRC (Canada) in conducting a research programme on primary mental-health care in Harare.

References

Blue, I. and T. Harpham (1994) 'The World Bank "World Bank Development Report 1993": Investing in Health', *British Journal of Psychiatry*, 165: 9-12.

Bourdillon, M. (1987) *The Shona Peoples*, Gweru: Mambo Press.

Chavunduka, G.L. (1978) *Traditional Healers and the Shona Patient*, Gwelo: Mambo Press.

Chavunduka, G.L. (1994) *Traditional Medicine in Modern Zimbabwe*, Harare: University of Zimbabwe Press.

Cox, J. (1994) 'Psychiatry and religion: a

general psychiatrist's perspective', *Psychiatric Bulletin* 18: 673-6.

Gelder, M., D. Gath, and Mayou, R. (1983) *Oxford Textbook of Psychiatry*, Oxford: Oxford University Press.

Kuyken, W., J. Orley, P. Hudelson, and N. Sartorius (1994) 'Quality of life assessment across cultures', *International Journal of Mental Health* 23: 5-28.

Lutz, C. (1985) 'Depression and the translation of emotional worlds' in *Culture and Depression* (ed. by A. Kleinman and B. Good), Berkeley: University of California Press.

Mutambira, J. (1989) 'Health problems in rural communities, Zimbabwe', *Social Science and Medicine* 29: 927-32.

Obeysekere, G. (1985) 'Depression, Buddhism, and the work of culture in Sri Lanka', in *Culture and Depression* (ed. by Kleinman and Good), Berkeley: University of California Press.

Patel, V. (1995) 'Explanatory models of mental illness in sub-Saharan Africa', *Social Science and Medicine* 40: 1291-8.

Patel, V., F. Gwanzura, E. Simunyu, A. Mann, and I. Mukandatsama (1994) 'The Shona Symptom Questionnaire: the development of an indigenous measure of non-psychotic mental disorder in primary care in Harare', in *Proceedings of the Annual Medical Research Day, ICHE*, Harare: University of Zimbabwe Press.

Patel, V. and M. Winston (1994) 'The "universality" of mental disorder revisited: assumptions, artefacts and new directions', *British Journal of Psychiatry* 165: 437-40.

Patel, V., T. Musara, P. Maramba, and T. Butau (1995) 'Concepts of mental illness and medical pluralism in Harare', *Psychological Medicine* (in press).

Saxena, S. (1994) 'Quality of life assessment in cancer patients in India: cross-cultural issues', in *Quality of Life Assessment: International Perspectives* (eds. Orley and Kuyken), Berlin: Springer.

Sims, A. (1994) '"Psyche": spirit as well as mind?', *British J. of Psychiatry*, 165: 441-6.

Staugard, F. (1985) *Traditional Medicine in Botswana: Traditional Healers*, Gabarone: Ipelegeng.

Stephens, J. (1994) 'A personal view of the role of the chaplain at the Reaside Clinic', *Psychiatric Bulletin* 18: 677-9.

World Health Organisation (1992) *The ICD-10 Classification of Mental and Behavioural Disorders*, Geneva: WHO.

The authors

Dr Vikram Patel, formerly Beit Research Fellow at the Institute of Psychiatry (UK), runs a community psycho-social health research unit in Goa, India. **Dr Jane Mutambirwa** is a Senior Lecturer in Medical Anthropology and Behavioural Sciences in the University of Zimbabwe Medical School. She is a co-ordinator for the Health Systems Research Programme in the University of Zimbabwe. **Dr Sekai Nhiwatiwa** is a psychiatrist working for the Ministry of Health in Zimbabwe. She has worked in mental health in Nigeria, the USA, and UK.

This article was originally published in *Development in Practice*, Volume 6, Number 3, in 1996.

Training indigenous workers in mental-health care

Jane Shackman and Jill Reynolds

Introduction

Hàns Buwalda's article, 'Children of war in the Philippines' (*Development in Practice*, Volume 4, Number 1, February 1994), describes some of the emotional problems of children in the Philippines, traumatised by political violence, and relates her introduction of Creative Process Therapy at the Children's Rehabilitation Center in Davao City. It raises interesting issues concerning the modification and application of a Western therapeutic model to a South-East Asian country experiencing long-term conflict.

We would like to explore this further in relation to the kinds of training programme that are currently being developed in former Yugoslavia and other areas of war or civil war. The aim is to train workers from ethnic minorities in mental-health care and counselling skills, to enable them to work with refugees and displaced people who have been subjected to war and extreme brutality, including detention, rape, and torture. All will have been affected by these experiences, and some may have been seriously traumatised. The training programmes and subsequent mental-health work often take place in over-crowded and under-resourced refugee camps, or in situations where fighting still rages, and basic needs for safety, food, and shelter can barely be met, let alone social, emotional and mental-health needs.

As trainers with experience in the field of refugee rehabilitation, we were approached by a British worker who had just been appointed as a Training Officer for a non-government organisation (NGO) in Croatia. Her main role would be to train Serbo-Croatian speaking workers in counselling skills and mental-health care for their work with displaced people from Bosnia. A psychiatric social worker herself, she had years of experience in the mental-health field, in various different settings — but she had no experience as a trainer, nor in work with refugees. She was clearly anxious about her role, and phoned us for advice two weeks before going to Croatia.

She asked, among other things: How do I plan and run appropriate training courses? What will the participants want to know? How do I find an effective way to share my own skills? Attempting to address some of these issues, we offer this article to everyone working in similar areas of conflict.

First thoughts

If you feel anxious about the limitations of your own skills and experiences in an unfamiliar context, remember that this may be how the participants on your training courses will be feeling. If you feel daunted by the task ahead, this may well reflect some of the fears of those whom you are setting out to train in mental-health work.

We suggest that addressing participants' own concerns and anxieties is a good way to start such a training course. It will enable you to identify more clearly their training requirements, and increase their confidence in expressing and asserting their needs.

It will be important to combine your own therapeutic approaches with the cultural frameworks and ways of working familiar to participants, so you need to become as familiar as possible (as quickly as possible!) with the local cultures, values, and situation, and take account of these in your training programmes and models of work. The participants on your training courses will be a rich source of information and knowledge, and they should be able to work with you to adapt ideas into culturally appropriate ways of working.

The selection of trainees

The trainees' own experiences, knowledge, and status within their communities will affect how they are seen and are able to function. Selection needs to take account of their standing and status within their communities, if they are to be trusted and well received. Primary heath-care workers or community health promoters, for example, will usually be known and trusted, and may be possible candidates for training courses. You may have little control over selection of trainees when you first arrive, but ideally you should introduce a sensitive selection procedure. Clearly the existing knowledge and skill-level of trainees will guide the design and process of your course.

Emotional impact of the work

In training people to work with refugees and displaced people, you need to address the emotional impact of the work on the trainees. No matter what ideas, training modules, exercises, and frameworks you bring, it is important to help participants understand and come to terms with their own mixed feelings about the work they are going to undertake. They are likely to have feelings of impotence and inadequacy, even sometimes of despair, as well as hopes, commitment, energy, and creative ideas. Acknowledging such emotions does not form a separate 'topic' in training, but runs throughout the entire course. You need to build in opportunities for participants to reflect on and talk about their own feelings about the work, and indeed about the training exercises you have asked them to do, and the feelings these may stir up.

The aim is to help workers to deal with their feelings of being overwhelmed or distressed. Remember that they are intimately involved with the conflict in ways that you are not. They are likely to share many of the losses and traumas of those they will be working with. That gives them both a unique strength, in understanding and empathising, and a vulnerability, in that the work may leave their own sorrows exposed.

In addition, clients can be very demanding, angry with workers who are unable to provide what they want, and jealous of workers' paid employment. The workers will have responsibilities that are new to them, such as assessing clients for propensity to suicide — and this can be a heavy burden.

Mental-health work is often painful and draining. The training should help workers to recognise their own emotional needs, and support them in their right to ask for help themselves. One Bosnian worker in the UK works all hours of the day and night, so that (she says) she can keep her feelings of distress at bay. She has no access to continuous support and supervision. This is one way of dealing with painful feelings that threaten to overwhelm us, but workers should be given opportunities to seek and receive support from others.

There are many ways in which you can pay attention to the trainees' emotional responses, and you will have to make judgements about how far deliberately to encourage self-disclosure in the groups with whom you work. If people have been working hard to keep their feelings of distress at bay, they will not welcome being stripped of their defences. Exercises and discussions which give participants the opportunity to 'put themselves in the position of the client' can be a gentle way to give recognition to participants' own needs for support.

An exercise on 'Asking for help' (Open University 1993) draws attention to the anxieties and loss of control that people often feel in seeking help.

Participants work in threes and each person is asked to think of a relationship with which there were difficulties. Whether or not they sought help in improving the relationship at the time, what difficulties could there have been for them in asking someone outside the relationship for help? When all three have discussed what might have made it hard to ask for help, they are then asked to consider what additional factors might make it difficult for refugees, or those who have been traumatised, to ask for help.

You can vary this exercise by making 'difficulties in working relationships' into the focus. It is in either case likely to give rise to some acknowledgement of trainees' own needs, and their feelings of ambivalence in seeking help.

Often clients will not talk immediately about emotional problems, but may discuss more practical concerns. Trainees can be helped to attend sensitively to these demands, to build up trust first, before trying to open up more emotional topics for discussion.

On-going support for workers

In times of conflict, normal support networks are disrupted or broken completely, and new ones may need to be built. Training courses give an opportunity to start this process. Allow time for trainees to discuss what kind of support they need, and how it could be provided. They may be able to meet together in smaller groups on a regular basis, if they work in nearby geographical areas; or they may ask the organisations employing them to establish a support or supervision structure. You will probably need to back up such requests by holding your own discussions with employing organisations. Burn-out is a real factor in this type of work: after a while workers themselves can become depressed, bored, or discouraged (van der Veer 1992), and support networks for them need to be established early on.

Create a safe atmosphere

If you can create an atmosphere of trust and openness, where trainees feel comfortable enough to share their anxieties, fears, vulnerabilities, hopes, and ideas, and to acknowledge the emotional impact of the work on themselves, they will be prepared to take risks in learning and trying out new techniques in working with clients. If you create a safe atmosphere, trainees will be able to make better use of any structured activities and exercises which you introduce, and to practise, challenge, and adapt new skills.

How can such an atmosphere be created? Think about how you will introduce the training course, and the way in which you intend to work. Proper introductions are important, and the chance to 'warm up' through non-threatening activities. We often use an exercise which combines elements of introductions and warm up.

Ask each participant to tell the group about his or her name, and what it means. Each person speaks in turn for a few minutes only. Participants will decide for themselves how much they want to share at this stage. If you start, you can set the tone for others. The exercise gives opportunities for people to talk about their ethnicity, family history, religion. It is surprising how much a name can mean to its owner and how quickly a few words on this can give others in the group a glimpse, revealing more of the whole person.

You can use warming-up exercises for a few minutes at the beginning of each new session: something light-hearted before serious business begins, and a chance for individuals to feel connected again with the group. Talking about something which they have enjoyed recently, or a memory of the last session, are other ways of giving each person a moment to say something at the start of a new session. Giving each person a turn is less embarrassing for them than if you put pressure on an individual to speak in general discussion.

Exercises can help people to think about issues from a different angle, and should promote discussion. A good approach is to move from individual work through paired conversation to small-group discussion. If people have had a chance to note down their own thoughts first, they are more likely to feel confident enough to talk to one another, and then to enter into group discussion. Encourage everyone to participate, using their own experiences and ideas, and value all their contributions. Acknowledge and deal with the emotions that are evoked. Give plenty of opportunity for participants to use their own case-studies and examples in their paired and group discussions.

Training methods

You may find that the way of training which we are advocating is very different from what trainees expect. Perhaps they hope you will present lectures, or teach more formally; whereas we are suggesting training that is experiential and participatory, with you in the role of facilitator rather than teacher. We believe this can be negotiated with the group, by explaining your training methods and the reasons why you use them. But you may need to make some concession to your trainees' preferences. This could be by giving some short prepared inputs, perhaps summarising learning and discussion from earlier sessions. It is hard for people to adapt to unfamiliar learning styles, and you will need to take this into account.

Participation is one of the keys to a successful training course. We believe that people 'learn by doing', and by reflecting on their own work. It is possible to achieve a high level of participation by starting where they and their communities are.

The theoretical underpinning for this approach comes from the ideas of Paulo Freire on popular education. Freire's literacy programmes for slum dwellers in Brazil involved people in group efforts to identify their own problems, to analyse critically the cultural and socio-economic roots of the problems, and to develop strategies to effect positive changes in their lives and in their communities. In effect, people teach themselves in dialogue with each other. Paulo Freire's advice on this process is relevant:

Every human being is capable of looking critically at his world in a dialogic encounter with others ... In this process, the old paternalistic teacher/student relationship is overcome. A peasant can facilitate this process for his neighbour more effectively than a 'teacher' brought in from the outside. Each man wins back his own right to say his own word, to name the world. (Freire 1972)

While trainees on your courses may hope that you are coming as an 'expert', to impart solutions to the problems with which they are grappling, you are more likely to be struck by the fact that you are working in a country, culture, and situation where your knowledge is limited. You may wonder whether your experience and skills are relevant. It is important to clarify your role early on: you do have expertise and techniques to share, but as a trainer you are there to help trainees to recognise and draw on their own resources and skills. You are there to help the group to tap their own wealth of experiences and creative ideas. We find that case-studies and role-play help this process.

In small groups of four or five, trainees can think of a real or hypothetical client they are worried about, or you can present a prepared case-study. After reading the outline of the case, and particularly the presenting problem, ask trainees to discuss in their groups (1) what do you **feel**?, (2) what do you **think**?, (3) what are your first steps going to be?, (4) how are you going to approach the client, what are you going to say? After discussion, trainees can role-play the start of the interview with the client.

Role-play should be seen not as a test, but as an opportunity for trainees to practise different ways of intervening, and to receive feedback about their impact and ideas about other approaches. Those in the role-play and the observers can swap places to try out different strategies. Linked with discussion, planning, and review, and done in a supportive environment, role-play can be one of the most effective ways of learning.

Cultural considerations

There may be considerable cultural differences between yourself as trainer and your trainees, just as there may well be differences within your group of trainees, and between the trainees and the clients with whom they will be working. You cannot assume that trainees understand everything of their clients' backgrounds and values, just because they are members of the same wider community. An examination of cultural expectations, values, strengths, and differences on training courses is important, in order to sensitise participants to their own cultural norms and biases in relation to their clients, and to encourage them to build on inherent cultural and community strengths in coping with losses, crises, and traumas.

Here is an exercise which can open up discussion on different cultural values.

Participants first note their responses individually to the following instructions:

- *List six values passed on to you by parents or care-givers.*

- *How did your parents or care-givers make you aware of important values?*
- *Circle the values that you consider to be peculiar to your cultural, ethnic, or racial group.*
- *Place a tick next to the values that you still adhere to and a cross next to those that you no longer adhere to.*

Participants then work in groups of three to discuss their responses (Christensen 1992). They may be surprised at values which are held in common, despite cultural differences, or at different interpretations of what values mean in terms of behaviour. They can recognise that most values are passed on by example and non-verbal means. Participants will usually identify the dangers of imposing their own value system. If the group you are working with share a common cultural background, this exercise brings out differences in emphasis, interpretation, and upbringing. This is helpful in cautioning trainees against assuming that they and their clients share common values and aspirations.

Again, opportunities for participants to think about their individual responses and to work first in small groups are important in giving everyone a chance to be heard, and allowing differences to emerge.

There is still a risk of inadvertently imposing your own cultural bias and value system in your powerful position as a trainer. It is not always easy to recognise your own cultural 'spectacles' (Finlay and Reynolds 1987). For example, your own professional social-work training, if rooted in Western, Anglo-Saxon, and Christian values, has probably tended to focus on personal, rather than collective, achievement, fulfilment and satisfaction, and to have valued independent thought and action. The individual perspective is not always central. Be prepared to have your own assumptions challenged.

An awareness of gender-linked differences is vital. How men and women are seen in their culture, and the investments they have in it, are not necessarily the same. Their responses to pain and losses, how they process these, and their willingness to express emotions may differ. Therefore you will have to give thought to how you might handle training groups composed of both men and women, and how you will deal with issues that may generate different reactions and responses according to gender. Sexual crimes, such as rape during civil conflict, would be a case in point. It may be helpful to give participants opportunities to work in same-sex groups on some topics, so that people have the chance to work out their ideas before sharing them with the mixed group.

Course content

So far we have mainly discussed the process of the group, and methods of training. We now consider some of the topics which we think you could usefully include (Reynolds and Shackman 1993).

Theories of loss and bereavement are central to work with refugees and displaced people. They will have suffered personal losses: the deaths of family and friends, the destruction of their homes, the loss of belongings; and abstract losses: certainly the loss of their familiar life-style, and maybe the loss of beliefs, ideologies, and hopes for the future. They will be uncertain whether some of these losses are permanent or temporary. They will be struggling to make sense of what has happened, to give meaning to the appalling events. An understanding of loss and bereavement can help trainees in their assessments. But you need to take into account that different societies have different ways of dealing with massive losses and grief, and have their own mourning rituals and rites of passage. These are often more collective and community-based than in Western society. Training should help trainees to recognise community responses and strengths, so they can build on these in their work. Many refugees

and displaced people feel guilty about the deaths of loved ones, and have been unable to grieve for them.

Crisis intervention is another theoretical framework which can be useful, so trainees can look at the more normal stages of transition in a person's life (such as adolescence, marriage, unemployment, old age), and how they are differently affected by unexpected crises or changes. Times of crisis are difficult and painful, but sometimes can present opportunities for positive, as well as negative, changes.

Training in *assessment skills* is a useful tool, in helping to identify what a client may need, and who needs additional help. Trainees can be helped to distinguish between 'normal' distress and more serious mental-health problems, so they can decide when to refer on for psychiatric help (a tricky decision, when specialist services are likely to be scarce). Trainees will be in a better position than you to know what is regarded as 'normal' and 'abnormal' in their own culture, and this should be openly discussed. The stigma of mental illness may prevent many people from coming for help. Workers can find ways to encourage people to ask for help after extreme suffering, without its being seen as illness, or weakness. A checklist for assessing suicide risk in clients can be useful, as can an analysis of the uses (and sometimes abuses) of psychotropic medication. You will want to raise trainees' awareness of the more vulnerable members of the community: for example, children, particularly those who are unaccompanied; women on their own; the elderly; and those with a previous history of mental illness.

An understanding of some of the possible effects of torture and trauma will help trainees to make accurate assessments: nightmares, lack of concentration, and flashbacks of traumatic events are often experienced by survivors of torture and trauma, but are not an indication of mental ill-health unless they are seriously affecting the person's ability to cope.

Workers can reassure clients that these kinds of symptom are to be expected after suffering traumatic experiences. If the person is unable to manage daily living tasks and interactions, this is a better indication than symptoms alone that a person is at risk and extra help is needed (Summerfield 1992). Often members of the surrounding community will be easily able to identify those whom they see as 'not managing'.

Counselling skills, and supportive, attentive and non-judgemental listening can be developed by practice and role-plays. Trainees can choose or be given case-studies or vignettes and can practise, for example, how to approach and talk to a person who is withdrawn and very depressed; how to listen and respond to someone who is extremely distressed and agitated; how to work with a client's anger and bitter hopelessness about the future.

Exercises and discussions that enable trainees to clarify their *role and limitations* are helpful. This was a topic that took up considerable time on a recent training course which one of us helped to run for Serbo-Croatian speaking workers in the UK, who worked with Bosnian refugees in exile. They were beset by demands from clients, colleagues, and their employing agencies. Becoming clear about their role and asserting what expectations they could, or could not, meet gave them confidence to say 'No' when necessary.

Other useful topics could include *problem-solving techniques, interpreter's skills, community development*, and *working with women who have been raped*. (Such women are unlikely to come forward for 'rape counselling', but might welcome the chance to be medically examined, and later may want to talk about their experiences or meet with other women who have suffered in similar ways.) Developing *group-work skills* is extremely useful, where numbers affected by violence and trauma are large, and where there is a more collective approach to dealing with grief and loss. People can gain confidence and strength from sharing experiences and supporting each other (Blackwell 1989; Shackman and Tribe 1989). Guatemalan women in Mexico City who met as a self-help group realised that they had all been going around thinking 'I'm crazy', when really they were suffering the effects of severe political repression and isolation (Finlay and Reynolds 1987).

You will probably think of many other topics: in developing the contents of training courses, you can make full use of your own professional training and skills. We suggest that you list all the topics you could cover, and what you think trainees may want to learn. Make up or adapt exercises to allow participants to try out new skills and techniques, and be clear about the teaching points you want to make. You probably won't use all of them and, once you find out the needs of your trainees, you will have to adapt your plans accordingly. It will help you to feel more confident if you know you have some ideas prepared: a selection you can dip into, a varied and filling menu from which you and the participants can taste samples. You will learn about new approaches and ways of working from the trainees themselves.

Constructing an interesting programme

Working with clients who may be traumatised and experiencing mental-health problems can be draining, and so can training courses dealing with these issues. Having a variety of topics and exercises will enable you to vary the pace and the atmosphere. Sometimes you might want to lighten the tone. Warm-up exercises can be fun, and can have useful teaching points. If you have access to video and/or slides, they too are useful teaching tools, which give participants a break from concentrating on themselves. Prepared hand-outs give participants reminders of key points covered. Summaries, feedback, and evaluation sessions at the end of each day will reinforce what has been done, highlight what participants have found useful, and disclose what the gaps are.

During the training course for Serbo-Croatian speaking workers we spent time reading poems, singing folk and popular songs from Bosnia, telling jokes, and drawing (they produced some vivid group pictures representing 'Being a Good Listener'). All these activities helped to build a strong group identity, and created a good atmosphere of trust and openness, in which many difficult issues were discussed and tackled.

We recommend that participants evaluate each training course at the end, so you can develop other courses from a firmer foundation. Ask for comments on different aspects, including your own style: if you can get people to write down some responses before you all disperse, this encourages some honest feedback.

Be prepared for the unexpected

Quite often trainers face the uncertainty of being unsure how long the training courses will be, or who will attend them. It is likely that you will be required to run a variety of different courses for both inexperienced and more experienced workers. In addition, you may perhaps be asked to act as a consultant to groups or teams of workers. This is a different role, and you need to clarify what you are being asked to do. Every training course is different, but we hope we have given you some general guidelines.

If it is possible to work alongside another trainer, do so, preferably someone who shares language and culture with the participants. It is always more productive and creative to work with a co-trainer, to plan courses together, to deal with difficult situations, to support each other. You will need to spend time developing a working relationship with a co-trainer, and even then things will not always go smoothly, but it is time well spent (Reynolds and Shackman, forthcoming).

Developing a model of training for the future

We hope we have given you some ideas and confidence to get started. As you continue your preparation, it is worth reading accounts of training programmes developed in Latin America which provide models of how work can continue to have effects long after your own relatively brief appointment is over. The self-help group we have already mentioned with Guatemalans in Mexico City developed a core group of female mental-health promoters who have continued to work with refugee women and children, and to run workshops for others for some years after the initial project (Ball 1991). A training model that reaches respected members of a community can have a 'multiplier' effect in ensuring that skills and appropriate methodologies are passed on to others.

It is important for the NGOs implementing training programmes in mental health to integrate this work into longer-term development projects. All too often, such work is part of a crisis response, when what is needed is commitment to supporting psycho-social programmes over a period, to give continuity with wider-ranging health and community-development plans. If you can raise these issues with your NGO at an early stage, you may be able to ensure that your work has far-reaching effects on the life of the community.

References

Ball, C., 1991, 'When broken-heartedness becomes a political issue', in T. Wallace and C. March (eds.): *Changing Perceptions: Writings on Gender and Development*, Oxford: Oxfam Publications.

Blackwell, R.D., 1989, *The Disruption and Reconstruction of Family, Network and Community Systems Following Torture, Organised Violence and Exile*, London: The Medical Foundation for the Care of Victims of Torture.

Buwalda, H., 1994, 'Children of war in the

Philippines', *Development in Practice*, 4 (1): 3-12.

Christensen, C.P., 1992, 'Training for cross-cultural social work with immigrants, refugees and minorities, a course model', in Ryan (ed.): *Social Work with Immigrants and Refugees*, New York: Haworth.

Finlay, R. and J. Reynolds, 1987, *Social Work and Refugees: A Handbook on Working with People in Exile in the UK*, Cambridge: National Extension College/ Refugee Action.

Freire, P., 1972, *Pedagogy of the Oppressed*, Harmondsworth: Penguin.

Open University, 1993, *Roles and Relationships: Perspectives on Practice in Health and Welfare*, (K663), Workbook 2, 'Focusing on Roles and Relationships', Milton Keynes: Open University.

Reynolds, J. and J. Shackman, 1993, 'Refugees and Mental Health: Issues for Training', *Mental Health News*.

Reynolds, J. and J. Shackman (forthcoming), *Partnership in Training and Practice with Refugees*.

Shackman, J. and R. Tribe, 1989, *A Way Forward: A Group for Refugee Women*, London: Medical Foundation for the Care of Victims of Torture.

Summerfield, D., 1992, *Addressing Human Response to War and Atrocity: An Overview of Major Themes*, London: Medical Foundation for the Care of Victims of Torture.

van der Veer, G., 1992, *Counselling and Therapy with Refugees: Psychological Problems of Victims of War, Torture and Repression*, Chichester: Wiley.

The authors

Jill Reynolds is a lecturer at the Open University (UK) in the School of Health and Welfare. She has provided training for para-social workers and community workers from Vietnam and other refugee groups and has developed teaching programmes on refugees in social-work professional training. **Jane Shackman** is a training co-ordinator at the Medical Foundation for the Care of Victims of Torture. She does clinical work with individuals and families, group work and community development, and co-ordinates the work of the interpreters.

This article was first published in *Development in Practice*, Volume 4, Number 2, in 1994.

The psychosocial effects of conflict in the Third World

Derek Summerfield

Introduction

According to the UN Department for Disarmament Affairs, there have been around 150 armed conflicts in the Third World since 1945. Twenty million people have died, and at least three times as many injured. In the 1950s the average number of armed conflicts per year was 9; in the 1960s it was 11; and in the 1970s it was 14. Africa in particular suffered a dramatic escalation in the 1980s, not just in the number but also in the scale of wars, some augmented by famine. In line with these trends, UNHCR recorded 2.5 million war refugees in 1970, 8.3 million in 1980, and currently about 15 million. If the internally displaced are included, the total doubles. Mortality rates during the acute phase of displacement are up to 60 times the expected rates. Eighty per cent of refugees are in non-industrialised countries, many of them among the poorest in the world. Sixty per cent of refugees in Africa receive no assistance.

According to studies undertaken for the International Symposium of Children and War in 1983, 5 per cent of all casualties in the First World War were civilians; the figure for the Second World War was 50 per cent, and that for the Vietnam war was over 80 per cent. In current armed conflicts, over 90 per cent of all casualties are civilians, usually from poor rural families. This is the result of deliberate and systematic violence deployed to terrorise whole populations. For instance, 'low-intensity warfare' (so-called because it is designed to carry low political risks for its progenitors) has been defined by a Colonel in the US Army Special Forces as 'total war at the grassroots level'. Population, not territory, is the target, and through terror the aim is to penetrate into homes, families, and the entire fabric of grassroots social relations, producing demoralisation and paralysis. To this end, terror is sown not just randomly, but also through targeted assaults on health workers, teachers, and co-operative leaders: those whose work symbolises shared values and aspirations. Torture, mutilation, and summary execution in front of family members have become routine. Recent events in Mozambique show graphically the staggering extent of personal, social, cultural, and economic dislocation which can ensue when conflict is pursued along these lines.

The psychosocial effects of extreme experiences

Human reactions to environmental stress have been subject to social and medical enquiry since 1900. It is accepted that individuals in all cultures may react to traumatic life events, usually involving loss, with disturbances of psychological and social functioning. Summarising many studies (though mostly in a Western setting), Paykel (1978) concluded that in the months following a traumatic experience there was a six-fold greater risk of suicide, a two-fold greater risk of a depressive disorder, and a slightly increased risk of a psychotic illness akin to schizophrenia.

For years it was assumed that the emotional effects of disasters, natural or man-made, were short-lived and minimal. This is clearly untrue. A study conducted seven months after an earthquake in Colombia killed 80 per cent of the inhabitants of the town of Armero showed that 55 per cent of the homeless and 45 per cent of primary-care attenders had suffered significant emotional disturbance (Lima 1987). In a study of the effects of the Bhopal (India) toxic gas disaster, 23 per cent of 855 primary-care attenders were identified by structured interview as having a definite psychiatric disorder (Sethi 1987). The best available comparison of baseline rates in the Third World is a WHO study in four non-industrialised countries which reported that around 14 per cent of primary care attenders had evidence of psychiatric disorder of one kind or another (Harding 1980).

Lifton's eloquent descriptions (1967) of the survivors of overwhelming catastrophe, like the Hiroshima atomic bomb, record how they found themselves changed; they experienced a bond with those who had died, and many had great difficulty in re-establishing trust in others. They had internalised a sense of their own worthlessness and powerlessness, like many survivors of great cruelty. Many felt themselves to be 'contaminated' with guilt, as if they could somehow have averted or mitigated what happened. This kind of guilt is not typically experienced by the victims of natural disasters.

Over the past two or three decades, researchers and clinicians have summarised what they saw and heard in survivors of extreme trauma under titles like *concentration-camp syndrome, war neurosis, combat exhaustion syndrome, survivor syndrome* and, currently, *post-traumatic stress disorder (PTSD)*. In fact the human organism

seems to have a relatively limited repertoire of responses to major trauma: sleep disturbance, lability of mood (including sadness and irritability), undue fatigue, poor concentration, and diminished powers of memory are common to all these formulations. These, I suggest, represent core features which probably appear in all cultures. We are concerned here not with transient reactions, but with enduring and frequently incapacitating states of mind and body.

A recent study of 57 Ugandan war refugees (Harrell Bond 1986) concluded that three quarters suffered an appreciable psychiatric disorder. Psychosomatic symptoms (headaches, general bodily aches, exhaustion even when not doing work) were prominent, as were clinical levels of anxiety and panic attacks. Three of the sample were contemplating suicide, and one had seriously attempted it. There was a close link between depression and the scale of an individual's losses, measured by the number of people in his or her immediate family who had died in the war. The researchers used a cross-culturally validated test during interviews, the Present State Examination. My own work with Nicaraguan rural dwellers who had contended with the effects of 'low-intensity' warfare in their daily lives for eight years revealed psychological symptomatology in approximately half of the men and three quarters of the women (Summerfield 1991b). Symptoms were similar to those in the Ugandan study. In El Salvador, at the height of civil war in 1978–81, psychiatric consultations rose from the eighth to the third most common reason to seek medical attention (Garfield 1985).

Anthropological interest in the stresses facing war refugees is part of a fifty-year debate on the relationship between mental health and migration, voluntary and forced. The literature has discussed the sources of stress in terms of loss and grief, social isolation, loss of status, and (where relevant) acculturation stresses and accelerated modernisation. Losses include 'home' in the widest sense, which includes the surrounding landscape as the repository of origin myths, religious symbolism, and historical accounts. With its focus on what has been lost, exile or displacement has been likened to a kind of bereavement process. These studies record considerable depression and anxiety, often persistent, psychosomatic ailments, marital and intergenerational conflict, alcohol abuse and antisocial behaviour, frequently directed at women. Single refugees, those from separated families, divorced or widowed women as household heads, and refugees in isolated situations, lacking company or community, have all been identified as being at higher risk. Some of these issues are particularly acute for those stranded in camps for months and years at a time. These refugees must continue to live with the awareness of a decisive change in their status, from active citizen to a marginal person — a war statistic. There is a pervasive feeling of ambiguity inherent in camp life. The future is uncertain and it is hard to make predictions. People feel incompetent and demoralised. Recent WHO-sponsored medical missions to Cambodian camps in Thailand further illustrate why such conditions are inimical to mental health (de Girolamo 1989).

War victims endure multiple traumas: physical privation, injury, torture, incarceration, witnessing torture or massacres, and the death of close family members. For example, Khmer refugees each suffered 16 major trauma events on average, three of which constituted torture by UN criteria. There are also background factors, not least the infectious diseases which flourish in the conditions created by war and are particularly lethal for children. In Uganda the AIDS virus has behaved like a terrorising army in its own right, and war-related social breakdown is hastening its spread.

Many studies have indicated that, as the overall severity of a disaster or war increased, so did the proportion of the exposed population manifesting psychological disorders. Pre-existing personality factors are obviously capable of shaping the way individuals handle such events, but when there is pervasive mental traumatisation across whole communities, the distinctions between individual and collective traumas may blur. In one report there was no significant difference between ordinary Salvadorean refugees and others who had been personally tortured, in terms of the severity of psychological symptomatology (Aron 1988). This also seemed true in my study of war-disabled ex-soldiers in Nicaragua (Summerfield 1991a). Similar observations have been made in, for example, the Armero earthquake disaster, mentioned above, and among the victims of politically inspired violence in Northern Ireland. But this area involves complex variables and many studies point the other way, like the Ugandan one cited above.

It is a myth, partly propagated by the slant of media reportage, that in the aftermath of a catastrophe people will be paralysed and helpless or break into panic-stricken flight, or that community function is likely to be shattered. Studies of populations under bombardment or siege in Lebanon and elsewhere have demonstrated low levels of psychological disturbance (Hourani 1986). This partly reflects the way in which emotional needs are overshadowed by the exigencies of immediate survival, at least till later. Human resilience is everywhere evident in the conflict zones of the Third World. Victims of wars are after all normal people, albeit exposed to abnormal forces. It is too easy to oversimplify the state of victimhood, characterising it solely by the psychological and social disturbances which can be documented in those affected. Victimhood is seldom 'pure'. Mazur (1986) notes that war refugees are not just hapless victims who have lost everything, but people who are conscious and active before, during, and after their flight. He questions whether they are actually helpless or merely labelled so. After all, refugees are survivors.

There is also the question of the effects of sub-nutritional diet on psycho-social functioning, which is particularly relevant in Africa, where war and famine have formed a lethal combination. Evidence accumulated from prisoners of war and refugees in World War II suggests that chronic malnutrition contributed to their psychological problems. Hunger can have pervasive effects upon mood, emotional drive, and social behaviour; famine has always been known as a time of violation of normal human ties. Undernourished children can be less responsive and less able to learn. We do not know how much this may add to the effects of institutionalised violence in a country like Guatemala, where up to 80 per cent of the children in some areas are reported to be undernourished.

Post-traumatic stress disorder (PTSD)

PTSD is a formulation increasingly evoked to describe the psychological responses over time, frequently years, following exposure to extreme and unusual traumatic events, commonly wars or catastrophes. It arose out of work with the thousands of US veterans of the Vietnam war whose unabating emotional difficulties blocked the route back to normal peacetime life. Since then, PTSD has been described in the victims of terrorism in Northern Ireland, Chilean victims of torture, Cambodian refugees and others. PTSD encompasses the symptom patterns described above in concentration-camp survivors. But most studies have been conducted in Western countries, and rather more on men than women. We know very little so far about the proportion of civilians of a particular population in the Third World who would react to conflict by developing PTSD. My pilot study in Nicaragua suggested that many of the major features of PTSD are not uncommon.

The characteristic symptoms of PTSD are thus recurrent, painful and intrusive recollections of the traumatic events, either in nightmares or in daytime 'flashbacks'. These may be intense enough to feel as though the traumatic event is being re-lived. A disturbed sleep pattern is typical. Another core feature is hyper-vigilance, often manifested as a tendency to startle easily, even in response to minor cues like small noises. Irritability, restlessness, explosive anger, and feelings of guilt, anxiety and depression may wax and wane. People may try to avoid stimuli that recall the frightening memories; they may feel detached from others, or complain of impaired memory or difficulty in concentrating or completing tasks. Sufferers do not generally experience all features together. PTSD does not of course represent a circumscribed disorder: there is some overlap with the features of chronic bereavement and in particular with depressive illness.

It should be emphasised that PTSD as a descriptive syndrome is generally not meant to include the intense but relatively short-lived emotional distress or disturbance which is a natural and immediate reaction to tragedy. Nevertheless, there remain open questions about what might constitute a 'normal' range of responses over time to experiences like being tortured or witnessing the shooting of one's child, and about whether underlying psychological vulnerability or the severity of the trauma is the central issue (Green 1985). The onset of PTSD can be delayed for months, or even years, and its effects can last a very long time: some World War II ex-prisoners still had symptoms 40 years later.

I suggested earlier that disturbances of sleep, proneness to anxiety, lack of energy, and diminished powers of concentration, essentially disturbances of arousal and drive, represented universal elements. What of the subjectively experienced emotions accompanying these indicators of altered body physiology? The emotional distress felt by a victim, and how it is acted out in daily life, will be influenced by individual characteristics, but also by social and cultural factors which help to shape the 'meaning' of the provoking events. For instance, guilt and shame have been prominent themes for US veterans of the Vietnam War, who came home to find that their society had disavowed the war and was somehow blaming them for it all. Those who had witnessed the massacre of civilians, or participated in the torture of captured Viet Cong suspects, have been especially prone to PTSD. There has been a powerful association between PTSD and self-destructive behaviour: since 1975 the numbers who have died (by suicide, alcohol and drug abuse, or shoot-outs with police) exceed the 50,000 who perished in the war itself. Men have had great difficulties in reassuming pre-war roles as husbands, fathers, and stable employees. In marked contrast, 50 per cent of South East Asian refugees in the USA display symptoms of PTSD (and even more are depressed), but there is no associated social dysfunction of such a violent kind (Molica 1987).

As its name implies, PTSD envisages the trauma or traumas as finite events, completed and receding into the past. But huge numbers of Third World people continue to be exposed to apparently unending war or State-sponsored oppression and must live on in the grip of sustained states of grief, fear, and apprehension. While such situations prevail, it is difficult to come to terms with loss. For instance, it is hard for a mother to mourn a murdered child properly while her other children continue daily to be at risk of the same fate. And while threat continues, hyper-vigilance, a core element of PTSD, is actually life-saving behaviour. I think we need an extended formulation of PTSD that encompasses the concept of continuous traumatisation.

I have considered PTSD in some detail, because it is so frequently mentioned in current medical literature. But clearly this kind of 'medical' model cannot address the overall complexity of human response to extreme violence, how people in a particular situation interpret things, how and what

they suffer, and how they adapt. These issues are further discussed below, in the section on culture and society.

Somatisation

Somatisation (or psychosomatisation) is defined, at least by Western clinicians, as the expression of emotional distress in the form of bodily symptoms. Characteristic psychosomatic symptoms include recurrent headaches, widespread bodily pains, un-explained malaise, dizziness, and palpitations. Such complaints are just as real and objective sources of hardship as those that might be caused by physical disease or injury.

Somatisation is a worldwide phenomenon. However, it has been regarded as particularly prevalent in cultures in which expression of emotional distress in a psychological idiom is traditionally inhibited; perhaps these are cultures which place a high value on interpersonal harmony and thus implicitly discourage direct expression of feeling. WHO studies in various Third World countries confirm that psychosomatic symptoms are very common. And published literature on the victims of war in Latin America, Africa, and South East Asia all conclude that somatisation is central to the subjective experience and the communication of the distress wrought by violence and disruption.

There has been controversy about the extent to which somatisation can be seen as 'equivalent' to depression and, further, whether it is a Western stereotype that denies the ability of people from non-Western cultures to express themselves in psychological terms. In fact, war victims with psychosomatic complaints often fulfil Western psychiatric criteria for depression, and some have PTSD. The dominance of somatisation among Asian patients does not mean that these individuals do not experience depressive feelings or have no psychological insight into their illness; but, some authors suggest, they treat those feelings as secondary to their bodily complaints. Other researchers have found that Indo-Chinese refugees readily discussed their symptoms in psychological terms. In Nicaragua I found that rural peasants clearly understood and expressed the fact that it was the stresses of the war which had generated their somatic complaints, little of which they associated with the pre-war years. Somatisation will also shape the kind of help that is sought. In Nicaragua sufferers were seeking Western (i.e. US) medication, an ironic by-product of the war. In Thai camps for Cambodian refugees, traditional folk healers ('krou khmer') have been effective. This is an area where complex psycho-cultural realities, not least those of the researchers, are operative.

Torture

Torture has been described as a form of bondage by which the torturer ensures that his interventions will last over time. Victims face the protracted psychological problems of other survivors of extreme trauma, including PTSD, psychosomatic ailments, and disturbed body image. The mere act of survival may bring its own guilt, and they must contend with a pervasive sense of anguish and humiliation. Like the survivors of Nazi concentration camps, they must endure what for some is experienced as a catastrophic existential event and rebuild a new personal identity in a world that can never be the same. They may also have lost parts of their body, relatives, work, status, and credibility. Spouses and children will have their own reactions. Reports from Chile (CODEPU 1989) convey what a struggle it can be to reconstitute family integrity and openness of communication.

'Disappearances' represent a form of psychological torture for those left behind, and this is intended. Only a fraction of the estimated 60,000 people abducted in Latin America in the 1980s have re-appeared subsequently, or had their exact fates established. It is hard to grieve properly for someone who may not be dead, and even after years many families are locked into what has been called 'frozen' mourning. Their emotional limbo is exacerbated when governments — even when restored to more democratic forms as in Uruguay, Chile, and Argentina — refuse to expose the whole truth about such acts, or to lift indemnity against prosecution of those responsible (who include doctors). Confronted by a State which holds on to its dark secrets and which seems still to insist that the missing are the guilty ones, it is hard for sufferers to overcome a collective sense of helplessness and insecurity.

Women in war

In the past the division of labour, the allocation of economic obligations within the household unit, and the elaborate protection built into the marriage system gave African women more rights than Western feminists assume. But the economic changes accompanying the colonial era (and continuing since independence) profoundly eroded women's position in society. Most of the responsibility for food production has come to rest with them. Throughout the Third World there seem to be strong links between poverty and households without a male adult. In parts of Central America, 50 per cent of households are headed by women. War, drawing in male combatants and disrupting social and economic patterns, brings harsh pressures to bear upon women's central role as provider of physical and emotional sustenance for children and the elderly. They are even more vulnerable when they must take their dependants and flee. Women and small children comprise more than 80 per cent of the population of many refugee camps and settlements. There is concern from various agencies, including

WHO and Oxfam, about sexual violence against women in refugee camps, committed either by other refugees or by camp officials who are in a position to apply coercive pressures. In the Thai camps, young Khmer women have been attempting suicide. Accepting that there may be gender-linked differences in the expression of emotional distress, several studies show higher levels of anxiety and depression in women than men following both natural disasters and war in the Third World. Women who have been widowed, have lost a child, or have been raped seem more vulnerable to depression and PTSD.

As a phenomenon, rape is linked to the dynamics of power and aggression, rather than to sexuality. It is endemic during war, and is arguably its least scrutinised and documented aspect. Though often seen as the random excesses of poorly controlled soldiers, it would be more accurately viewed as an instrument of subjugation and terrorisation, deployed on a more or less systematic basis. In Latin America perhaps the majority of women detained on political grounds by repressive governments over the past two decades have suffered sexual violation or torture, of which 'ordinary' rape is just one form. This has been experienced as an attempt to reduce the woman activist to the status of 'whore', a traditional symbol of shame in a Catholic male-dominated society. In the task of reconstructing their emotional lives, tortured women may face more social and sexual difficulties and be more prone to suicidal tendencies than other women whose experiences of brutality did not include sexual abuse. They may feel constrained to stay silent by well-founded fears of stigmatisation within their families or wider society. A recent study of 35 Ugandan women raped during the civil wars of the 1980s showed that years later most of them still had repeated nightmares about the event and felt angry, afraid, and humiliated. Twenty-five per cent now had no contact with men, and two thirds had no enjoyment from a sexual relationship. Three quarters of them had gynaecological problems, and some were carrying the AIDS virus. Half of them had felt unable to tell their partner (Giller 1991).

Children in war

'Low-intensity' conflict in Angola and Mozambique during the 1980s has demonstrated the consequences for the most vulnerable: the small children. Between 325 and 375 out of every 1,000 children have been dying before the age of 5 (compared with an estimated 185 before these wars), the highest rate in the world. UNICEF estimates that 500,000 extra child deaths have been directly attributable to war-induced destabilisation in these two countries during the decade. The psycho-social effects of unremitting violence and upheaval, here and elsewhere, can intrude brutally into the normal process of development for an entire generation of children. The stress and insecurity which all children can exhibit when separated from their principal carers, notably parents, is grossly exacerbated by armed hostilities and associated population movements. In Angola, for instance, an estimated 300,000 children have been orphaned or separated from their parents. They may have witnessed the harassment, abduction, torture, or murder of parents or siblings, massacres · and the destruction of their homes and communities. Older children may themselves be deliberately killed to prevent them being used by opposition forces; they may be tortured, or taken away for sexual or other forms of exploitation. There has been forced drafting of children into armed units in at least 20 countries on three continents. Worsening economic hardship may deepen their feelings of helplessness and insecurity. Children may be abused, abandoned, or neglected by parents or temporary care-givers, themselves under pressure. Uncertainty and tension in a strife-ridden environment intimidate indirectly, and thus the collective fears of parents and those of an entire society are added to the normal fears of children.

War-traumatised children in any culture are fairly similar in their emotional and behavioural patterns, which sometimes alter only after a latent period. Pre-school children may show frequent or continuous crying, clinging dependent behaviour, bed-wetting and loss of bowel control, thumb and finger sucking, frequent nightmares and night terrors, as well as unusual fear of actual or imagined objects. They may regress to an earlier developmental stage. Children of early school age can have these features too and be overtly unhappy, nervous, restless, irritable, and fearful. There may be self-stimulation such as rocking or head-banging. They may not want to eat, or they may have physical complaints — headache, dizziness, abdominal pains — with a psychosomatic basis. They too can regress to behaviour appropriate to a much younger child, in some cases to prolonged muteness or to bed-bound incontinence as if they were babies. They frequently have particular fears: of being left alone in a room or sleeping alone, or of situations which carry some reminder of the traumatic events they have witnessed. The social behaviour of traumatised children can be markedly affected, some becoming extremely withdrawn and mistrustful, others loud and aggressive. They may have learning problems. Adolescents can behave similarly, though their responses may be shaped also by whether they have passed the age deemed in their particular culture to mark the onset of adulthood.

War-related themes weave their way insidiously into the mental lives of exposed children. A study of 3–9 year olds in Lebanon discovered that war was the major topic of conversation for 96 per cent of the children, of play for 86 per cent, and of drawing for 80 per cent (Abu-Nasr 1985). The drawings of Ugandan refugee children show their preoccupation with their experiences of violence, death, and starvation: pictures of soldiers shooting their mothers, infants lying bleeding to death, decapitations, dogs eating human corpses, people crouching in the forests with ribs jutting and bellies swollen. A year later these children were still drawing like this, almost always from first-hand experience (Harrell Bond 1986). There must be distorting influences bearing upon the socialisation of the young in societies where force appears to be the only means of conflict-resolution, and where life seems to be little valued. They too may accommodate themselves to violence. Even very young Ugandan children, when asked about their aspirations for the future, talked of bloody revenge. On the other hand, a UNICEF-funded study of child stress in Uganda interviewed 74 who had been recently evacuated from the Lowero triangle, the 'killing fields' of Uganda. Only two identified with armed aggression, and the rest said that they wanted to help groups like the Red Cross who had helped them (UNICEF 1986). We cannot generalise.

In urban South Africa, politicised black young people often reject the norms of their parents, dismissing their pious hopes for peace as undue capitulation to the apartheid state. Perhaps what is being said implicitly is that parents have failed to protect their children from the oppressive State, so that they must now fend for themselves through activism, including violence. Thus it is that dominant authoritarianism can undermine benign authority, like parenthood. Inter-generational tension of this kind has been described elsewhere. But it is also worth noting that young people picked up at random on police sweeps may be less able to absorb the effects of arbitrary detention and ill treatment than those whose political understanding and commitment affords them a 'meaning' for what has happened to them.

A study of children living in the conflict-affected areas of Northern Ireland concluded that psychological disorders increased noticeably during the 1968 riots and violence in Belfast (Fraser 1974). Children aged 11–12 in conflict-ridden parts of the Middle East show an increasing incidence of serious psychiatric disorder, including psychosis and depression leading to suicide attempts. A follow-up of Cambodian youngsters, severely traumatised at ages 8–12, found that 48 per cent still had PTSD a decade after the events (Kinzie 1989). War can have an all-pervading impact on child development, on the experience of human relations, moral norms, and basic attitudes to life.

Culture and society

In the colonial era it was impressed upon indigenous peoples that there were different types of knowledge, and that theirs was second-rate. The emotional and social lives of subject peoples were defined in terms of European priorities, and the responsible pursuit of traditional values was usually regarded as evidence of backwardness. Subscribing to the prevailing cultural assumptions, and perhaps also to an implicit belief that mental ill health was part of the price that Judaeo-Christian peoples had to pay for 'civilisation', colonial psychiatrists thought that mental illness was rare in native populations. In the post-independence era, other psychiatric researchers have documented that depressive illness was common, for instance in Africa, and that anxiety in its various forms was as prevalent as in Western societies. But the relativity of knowledge is nowhere more central than in areas encompassing feelings, beliefs, and behaviour, and it has generally been non-psychiatric researchers who have emphasised the limitations of Western categories of mental disorder for organising our comprehension of what those in non-Western cultures experience.

Even concepts like 'stress' and 'coping' are bound by culture and, indeed, by class.

Culturally shaped beliefs about health, including expectations of the kind of help or healing available, determine to a great extent how distress is experienced, interpreted, and communicated. And though physical and psychological distress is experienced individually, it often arises from, and is resolved in, a social context. Shared supernatural beliefs frequently carry explanations and antidotes for mental ill health, though such attributions may of course provide a basis for the stigmatisation and neglect of the mentally disturbed. The social nature of illness, often obscured within individualistic Western societies, has been a major theme in the medical anthropology literature over the past 20 years. But despite the complexities of the subject, there do seem to be common denominators in human response to war and disaster, and there is the universality of bereavement as a life event, understood and dealt with by all cultures. There are similarities in the psychological symptoms and adjustment problems shown by Western survivors and by those from widely disparate non-Western cultures, as discussed earlier.

Major events impinge not just upon individuals but at the level of the whole society. Even if war-free, most Third World societies are facing rapid change. The colonial era initiated processes tending to the rupture of cultural continuity — the link between past and present — and these have been continued in the name of modernisation since then. Rural life has been depleted by the drift to the urban centres as the result of crop failures and patterns of unjust land ownership. That traditional family and social structures are under stress as never before is evidenced, for example, by the rapid increase of alcohol-related medical, social and economic problems in the Third World. Indeed, one study reported that 18–40 per cent of high-school students in Nigeria were consistently abusing alcohol (Oshodin 1980). The struggle between old and new forms at a time of economic stagnation must render societies vulnerable and volatile. Alienation in the face of Westernisation, which has not delivered what it seemed to promise, can arguably be linked to the rise of Islamic and Hindu fundamentalism in Asia, reactive revivals to reestablish coherence and 'meaning'.

War or civil conflict can be devastating for cultural and social forms. In Uganda and Mozambique huge numbers of destitute and terrorised peoples are haunted by the memories of the relatives they left unburied, and the supernatural sanctions which will follow these lapses of mourning and burial rituals. The civil war in Sudan has seen similar society-wide loss of ancestral places and social identity. In Juba none out of 36 refugee adolescents, all aged 16, could write a history of their clan. Many did not know the names of their grandparents or the village their clan came from. Not one could name any traditional social ceremonies. The traditional cycles of animal husbandry have not survived the generalised terror, and most cattle — the major currency for social and cultural interactions related to marriage, rituals, and settlement of disputes — have been lost. As elsewhere, women are left exposed. Young women from rural communities, where prostitution is unheard of, have been driven to engage in this trade in the overcrowded towns.

Trauma can spawn new forms of expression, or non-expression, which have in common that they defend psychic well-being, to keep terror and horror out, even if such behaviour is not necessarily adaptive in the longer term. Some of the survivors of the Cambodian holocaust of 1975–9, witnesses to the near-total destruction of their cultural identity, have coped so far by adopting what has been described as a 'dummy' personality, a kind of psychological withdrawal or numbing which allows avoidance of the past. Some say they do not remember what happened. Rural people in north-east Brazil have come to experience and express the physical and emotional responses to hunger, extreme poverty, and oppression through the metaphor of mental disorder ('nervousness'). This is a tragic rationalisation, but in a climate ridden with political violence, it may be safer to be 'ill' than to name directly the causes of their predicament. Chomsky writes that in El Salvador the collective traumatic memory of the massacre of thousands of peasants in 1932 was effective in suppressing dissent for over a generation. As late as 1978, whenever peasants began to talk about their demands, others brought up 1932 again. More recently in El Salvador there has been a striking resurgence of magic practice, from witchcraft to religious sects, among sorely oppressed communities who seem to need to replace lost 'meaning' in their lives. Messianic sects claiming a mythic invulnerability, most notably in Uganda, may be representing something similar.

It does seem that internalised cultural values and traditional expectations of family life and social roles are important in restructuring life after trauma. Adjustment problems in refugees can be reduced if they can join a community of others from the same background. This is also true if the culture of the host country is not too different from theirs, presumably because people in an alien cultural milieu are constantly bombarded by messages foreign to them. African refugees in exile are often anxious to revive their old customs as quickly as possible. In Guatemala, Indian leaders see the preservation of their linguistic and cultural forms (to the extent of keeping some of them 'secret') as paramount if they are to continue to resist State terror determined enough to have annihilated 440 of their villages in the early 1980s. Shared ideas about concepts like freedom and justice can obviously provide for coalescence within societies, as when the majority of the population support a 'just' war. I am in no doubt that many Nicaraguans were fortified against the psychological impact of the Contra war by what the revolution meant to them in terms of their history, and the new sense of a national self which it fostered. None the less, in Nicaragua and elsewhere, collective healing after conflict must be more tortuous when both sides have been drawn from the same society.

When catastrophes are as profound as Cambodia's, it will take decades or longer for a society to absorb what has happened. Those who till now have had to keep their memories locked must be enabled to find words to express experiences that were almost literally unspeakable. Some of the old traditions and beliefs will not survive this trial. For individuals, as for a society, things can never be the same and a new world view is needed.

Short notes for mental-health promoters in traumatised communities

Who are the most vulnerable? Members of the community are likely to have a good idea of those among them who are most preoccupied with their terrible experiences or who are generally a source of concern. Familiarity with the common presentations of traumatisation, for adults and for children, is needed. It is likely that people without family support, or women who have lost a child or spouse, are more at risk. It has also been shown that feelings of worthlessness, or the feeling that one is unable to play a useful part in life, or the self-perception of poor emotional or physical health status are all strong predictors of psychological disturbance in victims of major trauma. Social dysfunction like self-neglect or child-abuse is also a definite indication. These guidelines may also identify the most vulnerable children, because their emotional status during war has been shown to be strongly linked to that of their principal care-givers. Children can weather much more if they do not detect particular panic or depression in their

mothers. Further identification of traumatised children may be facilitated by asking questions like: 'Do you know any child who has trouble sleeping at night or who has disturbing dreams/nightmares? Do you know a child who cries a lot or who always seems unhappy or depressed, compared with the others? Do you know a child who won't talk or seems apathetic? Do you know a child who won't play with other children or who fights a lot or plays too roughly? Do you know a child who seems to act strangely compared with other children?'

What about emotional support and healing? In all cultures the healing process occurs through a system of symbols and rituals, verbal and non-verbal, which are grounded in the traditional belief systems of that culture and performed by individuals or groups whose role as healers is sanctioned by that society. Certain qualities of healers and the healing process have been universally identified as central to their efficacy, including communicating the expectation that symptoms can be relieved, conveying a knowledgeable manner, drawing together key persons valued by those in distress, and generating hope for an improved existence. A primary health-care worker or mental-health promoter who seeks to intervene in traumatised communities needs first to be acceptable to everyone and alert to cultural issues where they arise. A warm, sympathetic, and non-judgemental manner is essential, and he or she also needs to be clear that listening means bearing witness, and that this is not a useless activity. It may be very hard for people to communicate their experiences, and the worker, whether in a one-to-one interaction or in a group, can help to create an enabling atmosphere in which people can share not just the hard facts of their stories, but also their feelings. It is important to allow intense emotion to be expressed without a sense of shame. Signs of helplessness and low self-esteem may emerge, as well as the anger and guilt which are inherent in grieving processes. People may need realistic assurances that their feelings are normal responses to extraordinary events beyond their control and do not reflect personal weakness. Thus through discussion people can come to a better understanding of their feelings or symptoms, including the link between war-related stress and their bodily ailments. Groups, whether focused on discussion or on a practical task, also allow individuals to overcome the sense of isolation which so often accompanies serious emotional distress, and allow individuals to draw strength from the opportunity to give something of value to others. The worker can help people to talk through some of their problems, but should not offer instant solutions. Attention can be drawn to the ways in which people are once again bringing their lives within their control.

Concluding comments

Most conflict in the Third World currently involves terrorisation and deliberate attempts to produce psychosocial injury. Keeping this core psychological dimension in mind affords us better chances for accurate empathy with those affected, for tracing their responses over time, and of course for assisting in the processes of recovery and regeneration.

These psychosocial consequences are part of the record of what actually happened in any particular conflict, no less real or substantial than the statistics about the numbers of dead, homeless, and hungry. Psychological traumatisation is an actual experience, and victims everywhere need recognition of this. At the same time, I think we should focus on traumatisation not primarily as an injury which a particular individual may or may not have sustained, but instead as a *process* or *processes* impinging on social and cultural organisation at various levels: family, community, and society. Assisting a more complete counting of the human costs would be

consistent with the objectives of non-government organisations (NGOs) in relation to the enhancement of human rights and social justice. Further, the collective testimony of people who have been traditionally voiceless is also a writing of the history of the times. Wars create effects which can far outlast them, and follow-up over years is surely a priority. How will the lives of a generation of Mozambican orphans who witnessed the murder of their parents shape up over the next decade? Monitoring the effects over a long period should be a priority for NGOs and, indeed, of governments themselves.

The business of documenting is also a practical intervention. Just as the gradual recounting of the trauma story may be essential to the individual psychotherapy of a torture victim, so too assisting the process by which the traditionally voiceless come to be heard is of itself empowering. Naturally there must be no unmodified importation of Western psychological 'expertise'. Communities must be understood in terms of their own dominant conceptions of mental health and ill health. Given the variety of forms of co-operative efforts in the Third World, definitions of self-help will vary. Indeed, we are often dealing with dynamic situations in which traumatised communities actively evolve new forms of self-help and assertion. Community participation can be encouraged, but not prescribed. Local people must basically choose their own priorities and be empowered to act on them. The recovery of a sense of autonomy is obviously good for mental health. Thus projects aimed at psychosocial healing would invoke may of the non-material objectives of social development and education, as NGOs define them. With raised awareness, previously unanticipated psychosocial benefits may be spotted in apparently unlikely-looking projects whose official goals were quite different.

Human-rights bodies, churches, or any other organisation able to monitor and document the on-going personal and social impact of conflict need support and encouragement in this function specifically, as well as for the direct assistance they offer victims. And we need to be alive to the ways in which trauma-related mental-health work of the kind outlined earlier might be made available to a community, tailored to their particular situation. Mental-health training for primary health-care workers, the training of refugees as mental-health promoters, the preparation of audio-visual material which could be delivered in the schoolroom, clinic, church, or other facility are all approaches to enable individual and collective handling of the core themes: fear, unresolved grief, the problem of disappeared loved ones, stress-related physical ailments, alcohol abuse, abandonment by spouses, sexual abuse, and cultural threat.

One universal theme in human responses to extreme events is the crucial role of social networks in aiding recovery. Harrell Bond (1986) comments that aid has often not been applied to maintaining social institutions. War victims are expected to cope by being appropriately 'social', but may not have the resources to re-establish the real bases of social life. It seems fundamental that anything that can help to reconstitute family and kinship ties, and social and cultural institutions, must be good. There might be opportunities to extend the current range of social-development projects to serve these ends. For many peoples there is considerable reparative power in ritual, traditionally central to the struggle to retain the sense that there is order in the universe. Traditional healers can play a role here. There will be circumstances when early intervention, perhaps on a one-off basis, is needed: the provision of material for burial shrouds obviously qualifies here. There may be healing resources in other socio-cultural forms like music, drama, or dance.

Particular groups should be considered for targeting: orphans, the elderly, the physically disabled, those mutilated by torture. Women should be a particular focus

because of their heightened vulnerability during war and their central role as providers and nurturers, not least as emotional shields for their children. Projects that target women offer a way in to the mental health of the whole community.

The question of monitoring projects will not always be easy, not least because in the mental-health field outcomes may be hard to quantify. Moreover, in dynamic and often unstable situations objectives may shift in mid-project. Means of evaluating progress must be culturally appropriate.

If NGO field staff are to attend to this emotive and pain-ridden realm more closely, they may have to cope with higher levels of stress. They may also have to confront more professional dilemmas and even risks, particularly in countries whose governments directly or indirectly propagate violence, and where community health and social-welfare projects are regarded as subversive.

Postscript[1]

If the domain of psychosocial projects has emerged from increased awareness of the human dimensions of conflict, one unfortunate aspect has been the 'discovery' of 'trauma' and 'post-traumatic stress'. In recent years, trauma projects have had a sharply increasing profile in emergency-relief work, with their proponents claiming that huge numbers were affected, that local workers were overwhelmed, and even that such work could prevent subsequent wars by tackling 'brutalisation'. It is worrying that such expansive and fanciful claims could come even from consultants to UNICEF, WHO, and UNHCR. Trauma projects have attracted considerable funding, despite lack of evidence that war-affected people see their mental health as a priority issue, to be addressed separately from their other concerns, and still less that they would want it done in projects conceived and led by outsiders. It is a serious distortion to re-label the suffering of war as a psychological condition — 'trauma' — as if it were a technical problem to which a short-term technical solution called 'counselling' could be applied. Counselling is a cultural product as Western as Coca Cola, and is at odds with most non-Western psychological frameworks and concepts of mental health. There is a danger of perpetuating the colonial status of the Third World mind. Trauma projects ignore (and indeed impede) people's own traditions, skills, and approaches to crisis, and pay only lip-service to the priorities they deem most urgent. There is a question of power here. The current fashion for such interventions — not least in Bosnia and Rwanda — owes something to Western cultural preoccupations with emotional trauma, as well as offering a politics-free form of humanitarian work that seems to avoid the complex and messy questions thrown up by wars and refugee crises. In fact, the superiority of trauma counselling, of 'talking through' experiences, has not been demonstrated even in Western populations.

For the vast majority of survivors, 'trauma' is a pseudo-condition. Their concerns are not with their internal mental states but with their external social worlds, which have been shattered. The key issue is the role of this social world, itself a target in today's 'total' war, and yet still embodying the capacity of survivor populations to manage their suffering, endure it, and rebuild. I think the term 'psychosocial' is better dropped. The NGO community should aim to help people to strengthen and, where possible, to rebuild this social world and its valued institutions and ways of life. This means a social-development approach that acknowledges that each situation is unique and that indigenous understandings and priorities are the starting point. The emphasis of this approach is on collective experience. This puts a premium on NGOs interested in more than 'hit and run' operations. Related to this are questions that man-made violence, unlike some

natural disasters, always throws up: societal acknowledgement, reparation, and justice. Keeping these at the centre of operations may well be a test of the nerve of NGOs, not least in respect of their charitable status, but they cannot be ignored.

I have discussed these issues at length: see the annotated bibliography at the end of this volume.

Note

1 Added in 1996.

References

Abu-Nasr, J., 1985, unpublished paper, Beirut: Institute for Women's Studies in the Arab World, Beirut University College.

Aron, A., 1988, 'Refugees without sanctuary: Salvadoreans in the United States' in *Flight, Exile and Return: Mental Health and the Refugee*, New York: Committee for Health Rights in Central America.

CODEPU, 1989, 'The effects of torture and political repression in a sample of Chilean families', *Social Science and Medicine*, 28(7): 735-40.

Fraser, M., 1974, *Children in Conflict*, London: Penguin.

Garfield, R. and P. Rodriguez, 1985, 'Health and health services in Central America', *Journal of the American Medical Association*, 254: 936-42.

Giller et al., 1991, 'Uganda: war, women and rape', *Lancet* 1:604.

de Girolamo, G. et al., 1989, 'Report Of A Visit To Border Encampments On The Kampuchea–Thailand Border', WHO MNH/PSF/90.1, Geneva: World Health Organisation.

Green, B. et al., 1985, 'Post-traumatic stress disorder: towards DSM IV', *Journal of Nervous and Mental Disease*, 173:406-11.

Harding, T. et al., 1980, 'Mental disorders in primary health care: a study of their frequency in four developing countries', *Psychological Medicine*, 10:231-41.

Harrell Bond, B., 1986, *Imposing Aid: Emergency Assistance to Refugees*, Oxford: Oxford University Press.

Hourani, L. et al., 1986, 'A population-based survey of loss and psychological distress during war', *Social Science and Medicine*, 23(3):269-75.

Kinzie, J. et al., 1989, 'A three-year follow-up of Cambodian young people traumatised as children', *Journal of American Academy of Child and Adolescent Psychiatry*, 28(4): 501-4.

Lifton, R., 1967, *Death In Life: Survivors Of Hiroshima*, New York: Random House.

Lima, B. et al., 1987, 'Screening for the psychological consequences of a major disaster in a developing country: Armero, Colombia', *Acta Psychiatra Scandinavia*, 76:561-7.

Mazur, R., 1986, 'Linking popular initiative and aid agencies: the case of refugees', *Refugee Issues*, 3(2):1-16.

Molica, R. et al., 1987, 'The psychosocial impact of war trauma and torture on Southeast Asian refugees', *American Journal of Psychiatry*, 144: 1567-72.

Oshodin, O., 1980, 'Alcohol abuse among high school students in Benin City, Nigeria', *Drug and Alcohol Dependence* 7: 141-5.

Paykel, E., 1978, 'Contribution of life events to causation of psychiatric illness', *Psychological Medicine*, 8: 245-54.

Sethi, B. et al., 1987, 'Psychiatric morbidity in patients attending clinics in gas-affected areas in Bhopal', *Indian Journal of Medical Research Supplement*, 86: 45-50.

Summerfield, D. and F. Hume, 1991a, 'After the War in Nicaragua: The Continuing Impact of Physical Injury and Disability. A Psychological Survey in Two Communities' (in preparation).

Summerfield, D. and L. Toser, 1991b, '"Low intensity" war and mental trauma: a study in a rural community', *Medicine and War*, 7: 84-99.

UNICEF, 1986, *Children In Situations Of Armed Conflict*.

The author

Derek Summerfield is a medical doctor with first-hand experience of war in Central America and Southern Africa. He has been a consultant to Oxfam (UK and (Ireland) since 1990. He is currently principal psychiatrist at the Medical Foundation for the Care of Victims of Torture, London, and is a research associate at the Refugee Studies Programme, Queen Elizabeth House, Oxford.

This article was first published in *Development in Practice* Volume 1, Number 3, in 1991.

Financing primary health care:
an NGO perspective

Patricia Diskett and Patricia Nickson

The problem

Since the World Health Organisation's commitment to primary health care (PHC), declared at Alma Ata in 1978, PHC has been adopted by most governments as a strategy through which they could achieve 'Health For All By The Year 2000'. The aim was to develop appropriate PHC systems that would be widely accessible and sustainable at a level which poor communities could afford. *Community participation* (including participation in decision making) was identified as a key strategy through which PHC could be implemented. But this was often interpreted to mean merely *community contributions* (providing financial support and resources such as voluntary labour).

By the mid-1980s it was apparent that the costs of implementing PHC had been underestimated. It seemed unlikely that there would ever be enough public money available to meet all demands for health services. Many countries found themselves in severe economic difficulties, due to a combination of factors, including debt repayments, a drop in world market prices for cash crops, natural and man-made disasters, civil unrest, and military expenditure.

So, almost at the mid-point between the Alma Ata declaration and the year 2000, the issues of financing PHC assumed increasing importance. Many people still did not have access to PHC. State services were often underfunded, which led to poor supervision, poor-quality services, and chronic shortages of supplies, especially of drugs. It seemed that 'health for all' would remain an ideal, rather than become a reality.

Governments in the South found themselves under growing pressure to increase their investment in health, in order to meet growing demands on services and increasing health needs. Yet at the same time, the World Bank and the International Monetary Fund wanted those governments to cut public expenditure as a part of wider cost-saving exercises, often linked to economic readjustment programmes.

The conflict between ideology (health for all) and reality (acute funding problems, poor-quality services, and low coverage) led many governments to conclude that 'free' health care was no longer a viable option. Faced with this dilemma, they favoured the philosophy of charging for health care, for several reasons: it apparently provided them with a partial solution to their financial problems, and allowed them to reduce some of their commitments (or over-commitments) in the public sector. It lessened the need to face the harsh realities of re-allocating resources between and within Ministries. And it capitalised on the existing practice of paying for some health care through direct household expenditure (for example, on traditional remedies, private practitioners and pharmacies, and traditional healers).

Meanwhile, multilateral agencies, like the World Bank[1] and UNICEF, were finding that increasing proportions of their budgets were tied up in covering the recurrent costs of existing programmes and projects. This limited the opportunities for new initiatives. Governments were unlikely to be able or willing to take over these running costs, so recovering some or all of them from communities seemed to provide the answer.

It should also be noted that the renewed interest in charging for health care seemed symptomatic of current external (Western) economic policies, and was linked with the trend to push responsibility back on to the consumer. The support of external donors for the notion of cost recovery, through schemes such as the 'Bamako Initiative'[2] (see below), seemed to legitimise this trend.

While international donors were rediscovering the idea of charging, many nongovernment organisations (NGOs) and small projects were having to come to terms with some harsh facts. For many years they had tried to support their work through 'user charges' (charges for services) and community financing schemes, yet were unable to sustain projects at a level which the community could afford without continuing external support. In addition, many people, usually those most in need, would be excluded by their inability to pay, without exemption schemes and subsidies. It seemed that the international community had failed to learn from the experiences of NGOs and small projects.

There remains the chronic problem of funding government health care from public funds, in the face of growing needs and demands on services. At the same time there is an increasing recognition that many NGO-funded projects are not sustainable without continuing external support.

The Bamako Initiative

African Health Ministers met in Bamako, Mali in 1987, to discuss the problem of financing primary health care. They resolved to raise additional resources for PHC, but in a deteriorating economic situation few options were open to them. The Bamako Initiative was adopted, supported by WHO and UNICEF. It aimed to tackle some of the problems associated with sustaining and financing PHC programmes.

Specifically it attempted to address the shortage of drugs at local health centres and peripheral health posts. The idea was that income would be generated by imposing charges for drugs, and by introducing revolving funds to pay for drugs. The aim was to contribute to recurrent expenses such as drug costs, health workers' salaries, fuel, other consumables, and transport.

In its original form, the Initiative generated considerable controversy. There was concern that its focus on the sale of drugs would undermine the WHO's policies on the use of essential drugs, by encouraging over-prescribing and irrational drug use. This was a particularly valid concern in programmes where drug sales were linked directly to health workers' salaries.

However, the Bamako Initiative Management Unit (BIMU) of UNICEF has since revised some aspects of the programme. Despite its many apparent flaws, the Initiative was a pragmatic attempt to address a fundamental issue which still remains: how to finance and sustain health care in the face of considerable economic constraints?

Learning from experience

Concern over the implications of the Bamako Initiative prompted an international conference on Community Financing which was held in Freetown, Sierra Leone in 1989. Organised jointly by NGOs (Health Action International and Oxfam UK and Ireland) and UNICEF, it brought together over 70 participants with wide-ranging experiences, from those involved directly in community programmes to policy makers and researchers. The conference aimed to enable participants to learn from recent experiences and to look at key areas of concern:

- the Bamako Initiative;
- equality (equal access to health care for equal needs);
- alternative forms of health-care finance;
- community participation;
- problems of foreign exchange and the need for continuing financial resources;
- the rational use of drugs.

A full report was produced,[3] with specific proposals and recommendations, covering issues of concern for policy makers; operational problems in implementing community financing schemes; operational research needed for planners and implementers; and some practical suggestions for alternative forms of community finance.

Since the conference, there have been several formal and informal discussions and meetings.[4] However, there was a consensus that, while the Bamako Initiative had been designed to meet a specific need, the underlying cause which created that need had not been adequately addressed.

There is still concern that governments will need to make continuing and increasing commitments in order to address the health-financing crisis. Considerable support from external donors will be needed, on a long-term basis, if the burden of international debt, and the costs of maintaining services, are not to fall on poor communities who can least afford to pay. Cost-recovery schemes (recovering costs from communities) will at best be only a 'first aid' measure.

What then is the role of NGOs and project partners in the current situation? Let us consider some of the experiences of NGOs (in this case, Oxfam) which were shared at the conference.

Cost-recovery and community financing: the Oxfam experience

Oxfam's experience (past and present) is almost exclusively at the community level. It covers a range of different methods, including the following:

- fees for services given, or fee per consultation;
- drug sales and revolving drug funds;
- personal prepayment schemes (insurance);
- income-generating schemes (community or individual labour/fund-raising activities/festivals/raffles/donations, etc.).

The following observations are based on a selective review of some Oxfam-funded projects in Asia, Latin America, and Africa.[5] Oxfam funds approximately 500 health projects worldwide. About one quarter of them were reviewed briefly (through grants lists, documentation, and project files). Approximately 30 projects were reviewed in detail, through scrutiny of files, project visits by researchers from the Liverpool School of Tropical Medicine (to Chad, Zaire, and Uganda), and discussions with staff visiting the UK.

Charging systems

Many Oxfam-funded projects operate a variety of user charges, usually with a system of exemptions. Despite that, such projects tend to be regressive, for several reasons: first, the sick are penalised in relation to those enjoying good health. Moreover, the poor pay more, because they are at greater risk of being sick. When standard charges are used, as they often are, health care costs the poor a higher percentage of their annual income than it costs the wealthy. Thus some potential clients are excluded by their inability to pay. Where exemption schemes operate, their effectiveness is often not routinely monitored.

However, most projects using these charging systems depend on them for their economic survival. Many would argue that free health care would lead to poorer-quality services, or none at all, and that communities would be even worse off.

It is difficult to maintain a balance between recovering enough costs for the project to be viable and yet keeping the costs low enough to avoid deterring potential users. It is not possible to recover all costs if services are to remain affordable. Criteria for a more appropriate charging system would include the following:

- the development of an exemption system, agreed between communities and projects, which is then monitored;
- an emphasis on charges per sickness episode or consultation (rather than the actual cost of treatments or drugs);
- operational research (to investigate who uses/does not use the services and why) which can be used to modify the system in favour of the disadvantaged.

Drug sales and revolving funds

Many projects charge the actual price of the drug, with a percentage added on to cover transport costs, handling, inflation, etc. Others calculate a standard charge which can be applied across the board to all items; this may increase the cost of some normally cheap items, such as aspirin, in order to subsidise others, such as rifampicin.

The advocates of revolving drug funds stress their many advantages: the improved availability of drugs can lead to better use of facilities and improved quality of treatment; revolving funds, it is said, generate income and guarantee regular drug supplies; through careful budgeting it is often possible to provide free or subsidised drugs to the poor; and dependency on *ad hoc* donations of (often inappropriate) items can be avoided.

However, considerable problems are also noted. Calculating profit margins is complicated by management problems, such as having to budget for inflation, rising prices, foreign-exchange transactions, devaluation, import charges, and taxes. Many Oxfam-funded pharmacies depend on having skilled administrators to run them, and even then find themselves decapitalised after three–five years, due to such problems as those mentioned above, which are usually beyond their control. Another frequent problem is the opportunity for corruption at local level, especially when health workers' salaries are linked to drug sales or profits, and project or community control may be weak. Yet another problem is the definition of essential drugs and the prescription of non-essential drugs.

The problem of decapitalisation seems to be very common:

One scheme in Zaire developed an innovative and seemingly successful way of dealing with this. As soon as the programme had enough money, it bought cattle. When it was time to buy a new consignment of drugs, the cattle were sold. This meant that assets were not held in cash, which tended to lose real value, but in the form of livestock, which generally retained a constant real value.[6]

However, such innovative (and sometimes risky) solutions are the exception rather than the rule.

In summary, these schemes do seem to be successful in improving drug availability, when certain guidelines are followed. They cannot, however, be expected to subsidise other areas of health work, such as the training of community health workers, immunisation programmes, or preventative activities. Too much emphasis on profit would detract from the aim of making essential drugs available at low cost.

Criteria for viability seem to include:

- the development and use of a rational drug policy (including guidelines on how to use drugs safely and appropriately);
- use of a standard list of essential generic drugs;
- development of standard treatment guidelines;
- good management, administration, monitoring, and reporting;
- good control and monitoring at project and/or community level;
- staff training with adequate support and supervision;
- accurate price setting (which reflects the need to subsidise some more expensive drugs), or, better still, a standard charge

per consultation rather than per prescription;

- an exemption scheme;
- a guarantee of foreign exchange if drugs are to be imported.

Personal prepayment schemes (insurance)

This kind of scheme has featured more prominently in Oxfam projects in Asia than in Africa. In the projects, services are usually paid for in advance of need, which may bear no relation to service use. Costs are shared out among individuals, regardless of whether they use the services or not; so the healthy subsidise the chronic sick.

Oxfam used to fund Gonoshasthya Kendra (GK), the People's Health Centre in Bangladesh, which operated an innovative scheme. In 1976, GK instituted a system of prepayment which divided members into classes:

- The destitute/no male earner/disabled earner: these paid a registration fee of 5 taka each year, and 1 taka per visit.
- Families who could not afford, from any source, two meals a day: these paid 10 taka a year to register, and 3 taka per visit.
- Families who could afford two meals a day throughout the year, but had no surplus: they paid 25 taka a year, plus 6 taka per visit.
- Wealthy landowners paid 30 taka a year, plus 5 taka per visit, plus half the cost of the medicine.

Non-members could still have access to the services by paying 10 taka per visit and the total cost of the drugs or treatment. There were also different charges for a long list of services such as investigations.

About 25 per cent of those eligible were said to have enrolled in the scheme. Membership renewals, however, were quite low. Overall, GK recovered approximately 50 per cent of its cost, through fees for services and the insurance scheme (roughly 25 per cent from each).

There seem to be several advantages in such schemes. First, they are more favourable towards the sick and poor. Risks are shared, so the system is progressive rather than regressive. Patients are not penalised at their most vulnerable time, when they are sick and perhaps unable to work. As premiums are usually set annually, the project can depend on a certain level of income; this facilitates budgeting. Finally, annual payment of fees can take into account seasonal variations in members' ability to pay; for example, more money is usually in circulation after the harvest.

However, membership levels often remain low, because many people may be unwilling to pay in advance for a service which they may not use. In addition, it is not usually possible to cover a sufficient proportion of costs by this method alone.

In summary, this is one of the most progressive methods so far discussed, yet it is the one of which we probably have the least experience or knowledge. Some criteria for viability can be deduced:

- There needs to be good understanding of the community dynamics and community coherence, because some members of the community will have to subsidise others, with seemingly few benefits for themselves; considerable preparatory work needs to be done in the community before such programmes can be contemplated.
- Membership should ideally be broad.
- Premiums must be affordable, and ideally on a sliding scale.

Income-generating schemes

These schemes are often based on community labour. In one project in Senegal, villagers developed several different income-generating projects to support their local health posts and health workers, and develop water supplies. These included the sale of vegetables from market gardens, and the purchase of chairs and tables for hire at weddings and funerals. The latter involved the development of a women's fund-raising committee to control the finances and activities.

Such activities have made useful contributions to health programmes, but they cover supplementary needs rather than core financing. They all require a great degree of community participation, and in some cases have led to disharmony, with some members resented for not doing their share of the work. While fairly successful on an *ad hoc* basis, this is not a reliable method of financing, because it is difficult to sustain over a long period. It is, however, extremely useful when funds are required for a specific purpose, such as repairs to a health station.

Conclusions

It seems that most projects currently use more than one method of funding in order to contribute towards their recurrent costs, to purchase basic drugs and medical supplies, to supplement health workers' salaries, fund community health workers, construct and maintain facilities, and support specific elements of the programme, such as supervision costs.

Most schemes seem to have some mechanism for enabling the poorest to claim free treatment, although there is little evidence of the effectiveness of such schemes.

The most common methods used globally in Oxfam-funded projects are fees for services, and revolving drug funds. Insurance schemes and prepayment schemes are progressive and offer interesting opportunities for greater fairness, but they are few and far between. Other methods are useful as supplements, but will not in themselves generate sufficient funds.

Few projects are able to survive without continuing external support in some form or another, despite attempts to promote self-reliance. Projects whose main source of funding is one single donor are extremely susceptible to policy changes by that donor, and cannot always resist the donor's pressure to undertake activities which may

not be a priority for the project itself. One way to reduce this risk might be to develop a diversified funding base. However, external NGOs and major donors often play a valuable role in giving projects access to foreign exchange (sometimes their only access).

A possible role for NGOs

An underlying aim of many health and development projects is self-sufficiency. The theory is that projects have a greater chance of success when there is community involvement in decision-making and in community contributions. However, recent experiences in the health sector[7] support Oxfam's own observations that some degree of self-financing which reduces dependency on donors and governments is necessary, but total self-sufficiency is neither possible in the current economic climate nor desirable, because higher charges would be needed, which would penalise too many people. This is not compatible with the aim of equality, on which the whole philosophy of primary health care is based.

One option for NGOs is to make longer-term funding commitments to health programmes than has currently been popular. This will mean acceptance that some projects may need support and subsidies over a ten-year period, or longer, if they are to maintain their current programmes. It also implies a willingness to work more closely with governments on developing services in countries where infrastructure is weak, health status poor, and poverty levels high.

NGOs must accept that prevention and cure go hand in hand. While poor people may be prepared to contribute to the costs of curative care, it is unrealistic to expect them to share the burden of all preventative activities. These will continue to need subsidies from projects and NGOs. NGOs must also accept that sharing costs with communities (asking them to bear part of the costs in cash or kind) will continue to be an integral part of many NGO-funded projects. But total cost-recovery or self-sufficiency is neither a possible nor a desirable aim. NGOs need to develop clearer guidelines for field staff and projects, and provide a range of workable options which will protect the interests of the poor.

The option of free health care for all, while it may be an ideal, unfortunately would not be workable in the current economic climate, nor is it compatible with the policies of many governments, which must adopt pragmatic solutions to their economic problems. In many poor countries, 'free health care' means no health care.

The most appropriate philosophy for NGOs is perhaps to encourage cost-sharing between NGO, government, project, and community. This would avoid placing the burden of all costs on individuals, and would recognise that communities cannot be expected to provide the answer to current economic problems, but can participate in the development of programmes which benefit them directly. Emphasis on such cost-sharing will not address national-level inequities, but, if sensitively applied, can help to redress the balance locally.

It seems that NGOs have an important and continuing role to play in sharing information and the results of research; exploring alternative models of cost-sharing and financing; monitoring the effects of programmes on partners and beneficiaries; strengthening PHC structures and management at different levels, and promoting decentralisation in a hostile economic climate; and engaging in advocacy and lobbying alongside project partners.

NGOs which work with the poor need to retain a watching brief, monitoring the political environments in which programmes operate, and their effects on the poor and on project partners. They have a role in encouraging international donors to address the international issues and underlying crisis — a role which goes beyond merely applying 'first aid' treatment such as cost-recovery in the health sector.

Notes

1 David de Ferranti: 'Paying for Health Services in Developing Countries', World Bank Staff Working Paper No 721, 1985.
2 UNICEF Executive Board: 'Revitalizing PHC/MCH. The Bamako Initiative', Progress Report E/ICEF/1989/L.3; and 'Guidelines for the Implementation of The Bamako Initiative', 38th session of the Brazzaville Regional Committee, September 1988, document No AFR/REC38/18 Rev. 1.
3 UNICEF, Health Action International, and Oxfam: 'Report on the International Study Conference on Community Financing in Primary Health Care held in Freetown, Sierra Leone', September 1989.
4 Patricia Nickson: 'Bamako Initiative' (Conference reports), *Essential Drugs Monitor* No 9-1990, WHO, Geneva, pp. 7 and 12.
5 Patricia Diskett: 'Financing PHC: A Selective Review of Oxfam-funded Health Projects', internal report, Health Unit, Oxfam UK and Ireland, 1990.
6 Catriona Waddington and Patricia Nickson, Liverpool School of Tropical Medicine: 'Drug Sales: A Solution to the "Sustainability of PHC"?', paper presented at the Sierra Leone conference.
7 Thomas J. Bossert: 'Can they get along without us? Sustainability of donor-supported projects in Africa and Central America', *Social Science and Medicine* Vol. 30, No. 9, pp. 1015–23, 1990.

The authors

At the time of writing, Patricia Diskett was a Research Fellow in the Department of International Community Health, Liverpool School of Tropical Medicine. Patricia Nickson was a Health Adviser to the Christian Medical Commission (Geneva), and Lecturer at the Liverpool School of Tropical Medicine. This article first appeared in *Development in Practice* Volume 1, Number 1, in 1991.

Population control in the new world order

Betsy Hartmann

As someone who believes strongly in women's right to safe, voluntary birth control and abortion — and who is deeply troubled by attacks on that right by conservative forces — I am equally concerned about the ways in which population-control programmes can violate basic human rights and can be a form of violence against women.

The intensification of population control

In the so-called New World Order, the Cold War obsession with military expenditures is giving way to other means of social control. The ideology of population control is being refurbished, polished with a feminist and environmentalist gloss, and marketed with the latest in mass communication techniques. Summarising a Pentagon study of global demographic trends, Gregory Foster of the US National Defense University writes:

Already the United States has embarked on an era of constrained resources. It thus becomes more important than ever to do those things that will provide more bang for every buck spent on national security ... [Policymakers] must employ all the instruments of statecraft at their disposal (development assistance and population planning every bit as much as new weapons systems).[1]

Population control is also vitally linked to 'free market' economic strategies. The break-up of the Eastern bloc, the controlling influence of the International Monetary Fund (IMF), the World Bank and other international financial and corporate institutions, and the corresponding decline of national sovereignty have led to a systematic reduction of public spending on human welfare. Since the benefits of the free market rarely trickle down to the poor, then the only way of reducing poverty, the logic goes, is to reduce the number of poor people being born. If women have fewer children, they also form a better reserve army of workers for rapidly shifting multinational industries. Thus, in the 1990s we are witnessing an intensification of efforts at population control in both South and North.

Mechanisms in the South

In the South the main mechanisms of population control are the following:

● *Structural adjustment:* Government commitment to reduce population growth is often a condition of structural adjustment loans from the World Bank and the IMF. This is most recently the case in India, where government expenditure on population control is planned to increase, and international agencies are accelerating their efforts in the wake of an IMF agreement.[2]

• *Targeting population assistance at countries with the largest populations*: The US Agency for International Development (USAID) is planning to double its aid to 17 so-called 'BIG countries' (India, Indonesia, Brazil, etc.) in a move hailed as 'bringing a demographic rationale back into the program'.[3]

• *Rapid introduction of long-acting, provider-dependent contraceptive technologies*, such as Norplant and possibly the new contraceptive vaccine, in health systems which are ill-equipped to distribute them safely or ethically. In addition to targeting women and minimising user-control, these technologies, unlike barrier methods, do nothing to protect women from sexually transmitted diseases, notably AIDS. They perpetuate the notion that contraception is a woman's responsibility, furthering the neglect of male methods such as the condom and vasectomy.

• *Renewed pressure on governments to remove prescription requirements and dispense with basic medical standards for hormonal contraceptives*: For example, in a letter to the International Planned Parenthood Federation (IPPF), USAID criticises 'medical barriers' to providing hormonal contraceptives such as 'excessive physical exams (e.g. pelvic and breast)' and 'holding the oral contraceptive "hostage" to other reproductive medical care (e.g. pap smears and STD tests) ... With respect to contraindications,' the letter continues, '*we prefer not to even use the term*'... since it 'may have very negative connotations and a major inhibitory effect.'[4]

• *Mass marketing*, both of contraceptive brands and neo-Malthusian messages, through social marketing programmes and US financing in the South of popular performers, radio and TV shows, and media networks which neatly converge with the interests of pharmaceutical companies.[5]

• *Continued data collection and analysis* designed to persuade Southern officials of the need for population control. This ranges from simplistic computer graphics and presentations to the confidential 'gray cover' reports of the World Bank.

Mechanisms in the North

Meanwhile, in the North, intensification takes these forms:

• *Expensive and sophisticated lobbying and propaganda efforts* by population agencies, trying to attract increased aid-allocations for population control. European governments and parliamentarians have become a new focus of these efforts.[6] European women's health activists report that their governments' aid agencies are under pressure to change their relatively progressive stances on population to ones more in keeping with the UNFPA and World Bank agenda.[7]

• *Alliance-building between population agencies and mainstream environmental organisations*, which accelerated in advance of UNCED in Rio in June 1992. 'Because of its pervasive and detrimental impact on the global ecological systems, population growth threatens to overwhelm any possible gains made in improving living conditions,' reads a recent 'Priority Statement on Population' signed by many US population and environmental groups.[8] Such messages, broadcast through the media and local activist networks, fuel racist prejudices against Southern peoples and black communities in the North. Images of the population explosion are back in vogue. Dark-skinned babies are portrayed as 'mouths to feed', and rarely as potentially productive human beings.[9]

• *Immigration restrictions*: In the USA and Europe, immigrants are viewed as a threat to the economy, to white dominance, and even to the environment. According to Paul and Anne Ehrlich, authors of *The Population Explosion*:

The United States faces very serious and complex problems with immigrants from developing countries. The nation has traditionally said that it welcomed the 'poor and downtrodden' of the world, but unhappily the 'poor and downtrodden' are increasing their numbers by some 80 million people a year. Many of these, of course, would like to come to the United States or other rich countries and acquire the standard of living of the average American (in the process greatly increasing their use of Earth's resources and abuse of its life-support systems).[10]

The solution? Population control in the South, immigration control in the North.

● *Coercive population control of poor women, especially women of colour:* In the USA, while abortion rights are being seriously eroded, state legislatures are considering proposals to give cash incentives to women on welfare to use Norplant; courts in California and Texas have ordered women to accept Norplant as a condition of probation. An editorial in the *Philadelphia Inquirer*, a prominent US newspaper, suggested that Norplant should be used as 'a tool to fight against black poverty' and 'reduce the underclass'.[11]

The language in this editorial was so extreme that the newspaper was ultimately forced to apologise. Usually, of course, the language of population control is more subtle and seductive, a piece of Orwellian doublespeak which plays on people's genuine concerns about the status of women and the preservation of the environment. On the positive side, this language may sometimes represent a genuine change in thinking; on the negative side, it co-opts and obscures. To avoid that pitfall, I believe that feminists and progressives must constantly expose the contradictions of population doublespeak and clearly articulate our own meanings so they cannot be turned against us.

Population double-speak

First in the double-speak lexicon is the concept of **choice.** The difficulty with this term is that opponents of abortion and 'artificial' contraception have made anyone who supports access to them appear to be pro-choice. Thus, population agencies claim that they are expanding women's reproductive choices by developing and promoting new contraceptive technologies: the more technologies that are available, the logic goes, the more choices for women.

Perhaps the greatest master of this particular language is the Population Council, which developed Norplant and which is now promoting its use in countries with large top–down population-control bureaucracies. With input from women's health activists, eloquent guidelines for Norplant providers have been drawn up regarding informed consent, respecting women's request for removal on demand, and so on.

Yet the fact is that such guidelines are essentially meaningless in demographically driven family-planning programmes where women's needs have never been adequately respected. Examples abound of women being refused Norplant removal, as well as being denied adequate information and health back-up.[12] Is it technocratic hubris, political naivety, disingenuousness, or a combination of all three which makes population agencies so intent on promoting Norplant in systems where 'choice' is last on the list of priorities, and population control is first?

Interestingly, one of the new strategies is to involve women's groups and health advocates in the introduction and monitoring of Norplant and other new technologies. Referring to a series of such meetings, an activist writes that although they were ostensibly designed to open up a dialogue, their main purpose was 'to divine [women's] arguments, appropriate their language and finally exhaust them'.[13]

Although dialogue can be useful, women's groups must insist on their own terms as a precondition for participating. In particular, these must include the right to make dissenting reports, to be published, unedited, in the official reports of the agencies concerned.

And then there is the larger question: don't women's groups have more pressing work to do than to monitor the introduction of easily abused technologies in already abusive systems? Shouldn't the focus be on changing the systems themselves?

Contraceptive vaccines, which immunise women against a hormone produced early in pregnancy, are likely to prove even more medically and ethically problematic. Although one vaccine has been tested on only 180 women in India, it is being billed there as 'safe, devoid of any side effects and completely reversible'.[14] The scientific community knows very well that such assertions are false. For instance, many questions still remain about the vaccine's long-term impact on the immune system and menstrual cycle. There is also evidence on film of women being denied information about the vaccine in clinical trials.[15] Nevertheless, the vaccine is being prepared for large-scale use.

Meanwhile, the WHO Human Reproduction Programme is testing its own contraceptive vaccine. The chair person of a 1989 WHO symposium summarised the debate:

Foremost in my mind during these discussions was our difficulty in assessing the urgency of the demographic crisis. To the extent that the impact of that crisis increases, the need for more effective family planning methods must increase. At the very least, failure to develop something that might provide a more effective technology would be to take a grave and unnecessary risk.[16]

What about the grave and unnecessary risks taken with women's health? Genuine choice entails real power, not being on the receiving end of a system designed to control your body as a means of controlling world population-growth.

Another key term in population double-speak is **improving women's status**. Even the most die-hard Malthusians are for it, provided of course that it doesn't upset the global *status quo*. Female literacy, after all, is closely correlated with lower birth rates: educated women use family planning more effectively.

While trumpeting their commitment to raising women's status, many of the same people who bring us population control are bringing us structural adjustment programmes, slashing health and education budgets, laying off workers, raising food prices, and occasionally casting a few moth-eaten World Bank safety nets to catch the poorest of the poor. The result is disastrous for the health of women and children. The solution? Family-planning programmes.

Miraculously, family planning is somehow to lift women from their sorry status without having to make meaningful social and economic change. So, the argument runs, even more of the dwindling health budget should be spent on it. And, in the words of the Population Crisis Committee, organisations such as USAID should take care not to 'diffuse or weaken' family planning 'by shifting to a broad reproductive health or maternal and child health orientation ...'.[17]

Yet, despite their zeal to reduce birth rates, the population controllers leave many of the determinants of high fertility in place: the need for children as a source of labour and security, high infant mortality, limited economic opportunity for the poor. In the New World Order, even the saying 'Development is the best contraceptive' has an old-fashioned ring to it, rather like 'basic needs', 'equality', and 'human rights'.

There is yet another constellation of double-speak terms, including the **environment**. Preserving the environment is the latest ideological rationale for population control, even though the major causes of global environmental degradation lie elsewhere, in inequitable economic systems, corporate agriculture and logging, military and industrial toxic wastes, and inappropriate technology. Why are the rich always missing from the neo-Malthusian picture of the environment? Are they so invisible?

And then **sustainability**, a word so easily manipulated that in an article called 'Health in a sustainable ecosystem', Dr Maurice King can write in *The Lancet* that where there is unsustainable population pressure on the environment, public-health systems should not use oral rehydration for the treatment of diarrhoea in babies from low-income families.[18] Rather than indicting this argument, the editorial observed that 'Nothing is unthinkable'. The definition of sustainability must, in my view, be expanded to include moral sustainability. Malthusian eco-fascism is morally unsustainable, as are theories which claim that AIDS is a good thing, since it reduces population pressure on the environment. Such views exceed the earth's carrying capacity for racism and injustice.

My final slippery term is **consensus**. This is a favourite word of the United Nations Fund for Population Activities, which is proud of the way it has forged an international 'consensus' around the need for population programmes.[19] But whose consensus is it? I, for one, am not part of the grand UNFPA consensus.

Women and men need access to safe birth control, including abortion. But when family planning is designed and implemented as a tool of population control, it undermines health systems, targets women, fosters abuse, and perpetuates the 'technical fix' mentality which has distorted contraceptive research and development, and has led to the systematic neglect of barrier methods and male contraceptive methods, and a lack of concern for health and safety. This is not to negate the need for contraceptive research. But priorities must change, and women must have control over the technological process before research truly expands reproductive 'choices'. Within family-planning programmes, efforts at reform by improving 'quality of

care' are a step forward. But for the poor, there is not likely to be real quality of care until there is better quality of life.

In the end, blaming poverty and environmental degradation on population growth obscures the real causes of the current global crisis: the concentration of resources — economic, political, environmental — in the hands of an ever more tightly linked international elite.

Two centuries ago, Thomas Malthus put forward this analysis:

That the principal and most permanent cause of poverty has little or no direct relation to forms of government, or the unequal division of property; and that, as the rich do not in reality possess the power of finding employment and maintenance for the poor, the poor cannot, in the nature of things, possess the right to demand them; are important truths flowing from the principle of population.[20]

In the New World Order, the essence of population control remains this simple political imperative.

Notes

1 Gregory D. Foster: 'Global demographic trends to the year 2010: implications for US security', *Washington Quarterly*, Spring 1989.

2 See, for example, 'USAID offers Rs. 800 Cr. to UP', *Times of India*, 15 February 1992. On World Bank conditionality, see Fred T. Sai and Lauren A. Chester: 'The role of the World Bank in shaping Third World population policy', in G. Roberts, ed.: *Population Policy: Contemporary Issues* (New York, Praeger, 1990).

3 Tom Barron: 'New USAID population strategy aimed at "BIG Countries",' *Family Planning World*, Jan/Feb 1992.

4 Letter from James Shelton, Chief, Research Division, USAID Office of Population, and Cynthia Calla, Medical Officer, Family Planning Services

Division, to Carlos Huezo, IPPF Medical Director, 21 Aug 1991. Also see 'Paying for family planning', *Population Reports*, Series J, No. 39, November 1991.

5 See *ibid.* and 'Lights! Camera! Action!: Promoting family planning with TV, video and film', *Population Reports*, Series J, No. 38, December 1989.

6 See, for example, 'Europeans adopt population agenda', *Population* (UNFPA), Vol 18, No. 3, March 1992, .

7 Personal communications.

8 Contact organisations: Zero Population Growth and Humane Society.

9 See, for example, Paul and Anne Ehrlich: *The Population Explosion* (New York, Simon and Schuster, 1990). This book calls Africa 'the dark continent' (p. 83).

10 *Ibid.*, p. 62.

11 'Poverty and Norplant: can contraception reduce the underclass?', *Philadelphia Inquirer*, 13 September 1991. See Julia R. Scott: 'Norplant: Its Impact on Poor Women and Women of Color', Public Policy/Education Office, National Black Women's Health Project, for information on Norplant. The state of New Jersey has also passed welfare 'reform' legislation which denies benefits to children born to women already receiving public assistance.

12 See, for example, Sheila J. Ward *et al.*: 'Service Delivery Systems and Quality of Care in the Implementation of Norplant in Indonesia' (New York: Population Council, February 1990).

13 Personal communication.

14 'Birth control vaccine for women developed', *Planned Parenthood Bulletin*, Family Planning Association of India, Volume XXXIX, No. 5, November 1991. For a review of contraceptive vaccines, see Angeline Faye Schrater: 'Contraceptive vaccines: promises and problems' in Helen Holmes, ed.: *Issues in Reproductive Technology I: An Anthology* (New York: Garland, forthcoming in 1992). Also a forthcoming pamphlet by Judith Richter.

15 This is shown in two excellent documentaries: 'Something Like a War', a film on the Indian family-planning programme by Deepa Dhanraj (D & N Productions, 58 St Marks Road, Bangalore 560001) and a film about the vaccine, made by German producer Ulrike Schaz (Bleicherstr. 2, 2 Hamburg 50, Germany).

16 Quoted in Judith Richter, 'Research on antifertility vaccines — priority or problem?', *Vena Journal*, Vol 3, no. 2, November 1991.

17 Shanti R. Conly, J. Joseph Speidel and Sharon Camp: *US Population Assistance: Issues for the 1990s* (Washington, DC: Population Crisis Committee, 1991).

18 Maurice King: 'Health is a sustainable state', *The Lancet*, Volume 336, no. 8716, 15 September 1990.

19 Nafis Sadik: 'The role of the United Nations — from conflict to consensus' in G. Roberts, ed.: *Population Policy: Contemporary Issues* (New York, Praeger, 1990).

20 Thomas Malthus: *An Essay on Population*, Volume II (New York: E.P. Dutton, 1914), p. 260.

The author

Betsy Hartmann is the Director of the Population and Development Program at Hampshire College, Massachusetts, USA, and Co-ordinator of the Committee for Women, Population, and the Environment. Her published works include *Reproductive Rights and Wrongs: The Global Politics of Population Control and Contraceptive Choice* (New York, Harper Row, 1987; revised 1995, Boston: South End Press).

This article is based on a paper presented at the forum on Population Policies, Women's Health and Environment Women's Event, UNCED 92 Global Forum in Rio de Janeiro, in 1992. It was first published in *Development in Practice* Volume 2, Number 3, in 1992.

Adjusting health care: the case of Nicaragua

Centro de Informacíon y Servicios de Asesoría en Salud (CISAS)

We are approaching the end of the century, the date set in 1978 at Alma Ata for achieving 'Health for All by the Year 2000'. Undeniably there have been many advances since this goal was set. But there have also been enormous steps backwards. 'Health for All' seems farther away today than ever before. The conditions in which the majority of the world's population live have worsened. Structural Adjustment Programmes have had a dramatic impact in all spheres, especially in health and education. And Nicaragua is no exception.

Changing health policies in Nicaragua

The state of a nation's health is determined by macro-economic and socio-cultural factors, as well as by the provision and consumption of basic goods and services. Government policies, as well as levels of spending, are critical in establishing the health-care environment.

In the 1970s, it was widely held that economic growth would lead to an improvement in social conditions. The Nicaraguan government's orientation at that time was basically towards curative health care. In the 1980s, the Sandinista government aimed to incorporate health within an approach to social and economic planning that was geared towards meeting the needs of ordinary Nicaraguans. In its

first five years, there were unprecedented advances in the social sector. Between 1979 and 1984, the spectacular increase in health coverage resulted in reductions in infant mortality rates, deaths from infectious gastro-intestinal and respiratory diseases, and immuno-preventable illnesses. There was also a drop in the number of child beggars and female prostitutes. So impressive was this progress that Nicaragua's UNDP index of 'low human development' was up-graded to one of 'medium human development', even though economic conditions showed far from similar improvement.

From 1984, the rate of social advances slowed through what came to be called the 'survival period' caused by the Contra war, and problems were intensified by the economic adjustment and stabilisation programmes begun in 1988. Investment in the health sector declined, leading to a gradual deterioration in the quality of services.

The 1990s began with the election of a government which embarked on an economic programme to redirect resources towards the export sector, restricting overall spending, especially in the public sector, and rolling back the State. All of this was done within IMF and World Bank guidelines. While the programme succeeded in stablising prices, its results in terms of production have been mediocre, with high social costs and an equally marked process of exclusion. The per capita GDP dropped from US$466 in 1989 to US$405 in 1992. Even if the pattern of wealth distribution had remained the same — which it did not — more Nicaraguans would be living in poverty, and the levels of poverty would be more acute. Unemployment rose to 54 per cent of the economically active population, while the per capita consumption of food staples dropped by 25 per cent over the same three-year period.

The foundations were laid for a major deterioration in the nation's health: subsidies for basic services and essential products were eliminated; preventative measures such as the 'complementary food' programme were abandoned; and health services were generally reduced. As a result, morbidity and mortality rates rose, in particular among new-born babies and children under the age of five. Maternal mortality rates rose, as did the number of deaths due to respiratory and gastro-intestinal illnesses. By 1993 the UNDP re-classified Nicaragua as 'low human development', ranked 142 on the world scale.

Components of the health-care sector in Nicaragua

Health care is covered by the public sector, private business, and NGOs. But no real coordination exists among them, nor are there recognised national standards of service. The organisation and running of the health-care sector thus depend on the various participants' particular interests, with the State handing over more of its previous responsibilities to 'civil society'.

NGO participation, as well as the cooperation of multilateral and bilateral sources, was throughout the 1980s co-ordinated by the Ministry of Health (MINSA). Now, however, most NGOs prefer to fund community initiatives directly, or through grassroots organisations, thereby avoiding government involvement. A number of NGOs have emerged as an 'alternative' response at the community

level, in areas where the government has insufficient presence, or no presence at all.

So Nicaragua is virtually partitioned between government and non-government agencies, in which each defines its areas of influence as it chooses, or in agreement with the Local Integral Care Systems — created by MINSA to encourage administrative decentralisation. This lack of coordination, together with the limited resources available, seriously limits the chances of improving the health of most Nicaraguans.

Health coverage: a return to the past

The 1970s were characterised by inadequate health services and by insufficient human, material, and financial resources. By 1977, only 42.5 per cent of the Nicaraguan population had access to health care.

The Sandinista government implemented a PHC-oriented health programme, and in 1979 created the Unified Health System. The principle was established that health was a universal right, and health care an obligation of the State. As a result, 83 per cent of the population enjoyed access to health services, and 186 new health units were established throughout the country.

During the armed conflict of the mid-1980s onwards, much health-care infrastructure was destroyed, especially in the rural areas. The hospital capacity deteriorated, and by 1987 the ratio of beds per 1,000 inhabitants dropped by ten per cent — and has declined by a further nine per cent since then. Yet according to a 1993 MINSA Report, fewer than 70 per cent of beds were occupied, mainly due to the lack of supplies.

Access to health services today is limited not only by the reduction in public-sector supply, but also by the loss of free services, since the government introduced a cost-recovery policy. The increased supply of private services serves only the better-off, since the prices are beyond the pockets of most people.

Cuts in other social services also affect health. Government policy has been to withdraw support for Child Development Centres (which in 1988 served some 38,000 children), so that coverage has fallen by 23 per cent since 1990. The number of child street-workers has grown; some observers estimate that they constitute three per cent of the active work-force. UNICEF considers that as many as 700,000 Nicaraguan children are in especially difficult circumstances; yet the government has defined no policy to deal with the issue.

Charting the decline in health

In the early 1980s, there were major gains in the areas of infant and maternal mortality. In 1972, for instance, the infant mortality rate was 122 per 1,000 live births — a rate which had dropped by 40 per cent ten years later. Maternal mortality also declined by over one third over the same period.

With the problems associated with the 'survival period', fewer health professionals were employed by the State, and larger numbers of children were not covered by immunisation programmes. Increased poverty and hardship, and the widespread lack of access to safe drinking water, leave people more vulnerable to illness.

But according to MINSA's records, maternal mortality has soared since then. Today, one in every 66 women of child-bearing age dies due to complications related to pregnancy or childbirth. For rich countries, the figure is one in every 10,000. Infant mortality has also begun to rise, and in some districts stands at 138 per 1,000 live births among illiterate mothers: six times higher than the index among mothers who have completed primary, secondary, or further education. Given that illiteracy has risen since 1989, the likely consequences are all too obvious.

Nicaraguans are ever less likely to seek medical or dental treatment, and preventative health programmes have also been cut

back. For example, immunisations for the major preventable diseases such as measles, diphtheria, and tetanus dropped by 61 per cent, 23 per cent, and 44 per cent respectively between 1988 and 1994. According to a survey by PROFAMILIA (*Salud Familiar, Nicaragua 92-93*), only 27 per cent of children are fully immunised before they are one year old. Deaths due to immuno-preventable diseases are rising, as are those caused by gastro-intestinal illnesses. Malnutrition is now a major secondary cause of childhood death.

Finally, Nicaragua has seen a disturbing increase in the number of deaths from violent causes. Between 1988 and 1992, crimes against individuals and drug-related offences grew by 66 per cent and 96 per cent respectively. The number of homicides went up by a massive 385 per cent. Unemployment and alcohol are, according to a police report on the subject, common denominators.

Paying for health, and paying for sickness

In the early years of the Sandinista government, national spending on health (both current spending and investment) steadily increased; though, as we saw above, it declined from the mid-1980s. This downward trend has continued: per capita spending on health fell from US$63 in 1988 to US$44 in 1992.

According to a 1993 World Bank diagnosis, most of Nicaragua's existing medical equipment was already at the end of its useful life, and almost half was unreliable or out of order. Almost all hospitals required major repairs, and four needed to be replaced.

In Nicaragua, the 'enabling State' is a cosmetic term which conceals the government's abrogation of its responsibilities for health. The population has been abandoned to its fate. Private spending has grown, mainly in out-patient care — and, of course, mainly in the capital city. It does not reach low-income groups, and it does not serve the needs of anyone unable to travel to Managua.

NGO spending has increased by 48 per cent since 1988. But while this is a significant trend, the amount is insignificant in terms of the cost of maintaining national health-care provision.

Putting health into perspective

What we have shown is not a pretty picture. The panorama seems grim. According to some, Nicaragua has already reached rock-bottom: things can only improve. While the situation is so bad that it is hard to imagine it getting any worse, we cannot afford to assume that things will get better. If we do not take concrete steps to counteract the effects of Structural Adjustment Programmes in eroding health-care provision, the situation will continue to deteriorate.

We cannot talk about sustainable social and human development without there also being a commitment — backed up with action — to change the structures that promote and perpetuate inequity and injustice, and unless health care is designed to be accessible to every citizen. Both governments and organised civil society have a responsibility to meet these challenges. *Human development and economic growth cannot be seen as separate from each other.* Access to basic services, among them health, is a fundamental right of all people.

While the unjust policies and structures at an international level are very important obstacles to achieving social and economic development, it is not enough merely to reform them. We also have to make radical changes within our own countries to assure the full participation of all members of our societies, and their just and equitable access to resources and services.

A major challenge facing civil society in general — in particular movements representing ordinary people — is to participate in drafting our countries' social and economic policies so that sustainable *human* development is genuinely promoted.

The Alma Ata recommendations should be taken up again. These include the incorporation of health within an integral, multi-disciplinary, and multi-sectoral approach to social planning. For this to happen, more of us need to have a clear and comprehensive picture of the situation, so that we can build this into our demands and proposals. Above all, we need to ensure that people have the chance to express their views, and fight for these to be taken into account in the agreements, policies, and plans both of governments and of international financial institutions.

Note

This article is adapted from *La salud y los ajustes estructurales en Nicaragua* (available in English as *Health and Structural Adjustment in Nicaragua*), published in February 1995 by the Centro de Información y Servicios de Asesoría en Salud (CISAS) for the World Summit on Social Development. Statistics are taken from official government documents, unless other sources are cited.

The author

CISAS is a Nicaraguan NGO dedicated to grassroots education and social communication about health.

The article synthesises research by Dr Edmundo Sánchez of the Centro de Investigaciones y Estudios de la Salud of the Nicaraguan School of Public Health. It was first published in *Development in Practice* Volume 5, Number 4, in 1995.

Evaluating HIV/AIDS programmes

Hilary Hughes

What is a successful HIV/AIDS intervention? This may sound like the million-dollar question in AIDS prevention, but it need not be. Answers can be found, if we are clear who is asking the question, and why.

First, we must define our objectives. What can we realistically expect any HIV/AIDS intervention to achieve? Most AIDS-control programmes share the same fundamental aim: to reduce the spread of HIV through promotion of safer sexual behaviour. This is a long-term objective, requiring deep-rooted social change. Evaluating the success of projects in the short term by looking at longer-term indications — such as sustained changes in sexual behaviour — can be demoralising and misleading: demoralising, because to expect that long-term goals can immediately be achieved will often lead to a hopeless sense of failure; misleading, because those changes which can be observed cannot be attributed to any particular project or activity, since behaviours are affected by a range of external factors, from migration to mass media.

The lessons so far

Despite difficulties in evaluating results in the short term, we have learnt important lessons about successful promotion of safer sex. Before AIDS became a major public-health concern, health-education workers already knew what helps to change behaviour — such as avoiding unwanted pregnancy or stopping smoking — and what does not. Later, those working in HIV/AIDS-specific programmes were to learn many of the same lessons, but only after valuable time had already been lost.

We know that information alone is insufficient to change behaviour. Information directed from outside through leaflets, talks, or mass media and marketing campaigns towards individual members of the public or target groups is not enough for them to act on it. People are most likely to change when those around them are changing. In the case of sexual behaviour, they change because their sexual partners are changing: it does, after all, take at least two to have safer sex! Encouragement of sustained, inter-personal communication and 'peer' pressure are, therefore, fundamental.

We could take as an example the way in which an existing community-based primary health-care (PHC) clinic, set up by a Residents' Association in Rocinha, Rio de Janeiro, integrated AIDS-prevention work into its activities. This local health post was already providing medical care to over 5,000 households, as well as promoting a participatory response to common health problems such as scabies and measles. The work is inter-sectoral and inter-disciplinary, involving residents, local and national media, and local and national government.

Four years after diagnosing its first AIDS patient in 1987, this same PHC programme had set up and trained an extensive network of volunteer AIDS counsellors/educators in the community, as well as a system of free, targeted distribution of condoms, monitoring their use through the inter-personal contact of the AIDS educators. The project has improved medical assistance to those with HIV disease, improved relations with local State HIV-testing services, and established qualitative and quantitative monitoring and evaluation of all programme activities.

Mass media and public educational campaigns on AIDS prevention were also launched, including local radio programmes, a video production featuring interviews with residents on their views about AIDS, a school play, and a popular dance (*lambada*). This illustrates ways of enhancing peer pressure and inter-personal communication: people are more likely to act on the information they receive in one sphere if the same messages are reinforced through other channels in their lives, such as radio, film, and discos.

The success of this programme is largely due to the pre-existence of the health post and its commitment to encouraging participatory peer education in the community, as well as encouraging an integrated, inter-sectoral response, involving mass media and local government.

How does an HIV/AIDS intervention begin this process? We must first find a 'point of entry' in any particular group or community at risk. This means that we need to find out how to make AIDS, or any other sexual-health issue, relevant. To persuade people that HIV/AIDS is important, the topic must be addressed in the context of those issues which are of more immediate concern: to a street child in Brazil, this is surviving daily violence; to a woman selling sex in a bar in Nairobi, it may be feeding her children; to a migrant agricultural worker on the US/Mexican border, it may be poverty, pesticides, and

lack of water. Within this context, there are always some individuals who have influence within a group. This may be the local gang leader of street youth in Rio de Janeiro, or a national leader of the Brazilian Movement of Street Boys and Girls, working to defend the civil rights of all young people living on the streets. Among migrant workers, it may be a labour leader, or a leader of an ethnic minority which forms part of the migrant labour force. These people can use their position to integrate the issue of sexual health within their everyday community-development work. In this case, the issue is to encourage more open discussion on the topic of sexual pleasure and disease prevention.

The success of any AIDS programme is crucially related to the level of organisation already in existence before work on AIDS commences. The degree to which people at risk are already organised determines the effectiveness of their channels for communication and action. For example, the success of the Rocinha AIDS programme is largely due to the pre-existence of the health post already set up and run by the local Residents' Association.

The opposite is also true: the more vulnerable, isolated, and marginalised people are, the less likely it is that they will be able to change their behaviour and act on the knowledge that they are at risk of HIV. This necessarily means that the political organisation of vulnerable people to act confidently in their own interests and to articulate their concerns must form the broader objectives of any AIDS intervention. Such objectives must, therefore, be taken into account when evaluating the success of any particular project.

Success — in whose eyes?

How can we evaluate a project whose wider objectives include empowerment and leadership development? Take, for example, a project focusing on sex-workers, or prostitutes. The initial objective, as agreed by the funders, is to set up a centre focusing on safer-sex counselling and free distribution of condoms. Attendance at the centre is at first minimal. The women's more immediate concerns include fear of violent and abusive clients, many of them frequent offenders. As the centre becomes a meeting place for sex-workers, discussion leads to action; and the women develop and up-date a descriptive database on dangerous clients, known as the 'Ugly Mugs' file. Six months later, a survey reveals that most women come to the centre primarily to pick up the latest 'Ugly Mugs' information, rather than the condoms. In the eyes of the sex-workers, this project is a 'success'. The women feel more confident not only about avoiding dangerous clients, but also about collectively demanding 'No condoms —- no sex'. The funders, however, are more keen to ensure that their funds are spent specifically on promoting condoms, rather than on a 'social centre' for sex-workers.

Given the complex factors which influence sexual behaviour, a project may change its short-term objectives and/or strategies, still with the same longer-term goals in mind. This is true of many health-related initiatives, which begin with specific aims and are then forced to confront far broader social issues. Where funders and project workers begin to differ in their proposed objectives, they will also differ in the evaluation indicators chosen.

Indicating social change

One answer to this problem is to select indicators, from the start, which reflect the broader social issues that any HIV/AIDS project can expect to confront; and which are flexible enough to reflect the changing reality of the project. For example, in the sex-worker project cited above, this would entail finding ways to measure the women's increased confidence to act collectively in their own interest.

Unfortunately, indicators are often selected not because they are the most appropriate, but because they are the easiest to measure; for example, tracking the number of condoms distributed, as opposed to assessing the increased likelihood that these will, or can, be used for their intended purpose. Indicators should be creatively set, using both qualitative and quantitative data as appropriate. For example, a quantitative evaluation of a project working with adolescents in Mexico, based on a statistical analysis of responses to a written questionnaire, seemed to indicate that educational work on AIDS had caused more adolescents to believe that contraceptives were difficult to obtain. Further qualitative investigation (focus-group interviews) revealed that, as a result of the educational programme, more adolescents had attempted to buy condoms — a positive outcome — but in doing so had discovered that many chemists did not stock them — a broader social problem which the programme would have to find ways of addressing.

Although there is no single way to evaluate 'success', we can develop better ways of monitoring our achievements and failures, on both an individual and a collective basis:

• More effective information-exchange on the results of simple approaches to project-evaluation will help similar projects to improve current activities, and learn from past mistakes — so long as realistic objectives are set in the first place. Stated objectives and indicators should broadly reflect key aspects of the project's social and political context. Questions to ask in a evaluation are then surprisingly simple: are the stated aims and objectives being met? How is this being achieved? Simple research techniques include comparative studies of a group of people involved in any activity and a similar group which is not; and questionnaire surveys on the effect of project activities on participants.

• Small-scale research into current sexual practices, and *monitoring* changes, can be used to inform project activities (although this cannot be used as a measure of an individual project's success). For example, community educators in Zambia promoting marital fidelity have used local Chief's Council records of assault cases as an indicator of the incidence of sex outside marriage, since 'most assault cases are the result of one man sleeping with another man's wife'. An apparent decrease in these cases has encouraged continued promotion of marital fidelity as one approach to reducing high-risk behaviour.

• Improved communication between site-specific projects and larger research programmes can help us to better relate the aims and objectives of small-scale projects to our collective, longer-term goals, i.e. sustained behavioural change and reduced spread of HIV. For example, large epidemiological and behavioural research programmes should ensure that all sexual health projects operating in the areas under investigation are informed of the results and of their implications.

• Many projects currently operate within a two–three year funding cycle. Projects should be encouraged to operate within more appropriate time-frames, given the longer-term nature of the ultimate goals.

In conclusion, there is one crucial lesson that we do not have time to re-learn. Community workers around the world recognise that health promotion requires deep-rooted social change. Sexual health is no different. In measuring the success of an HIV/AIDS intervention, therefore, one of the most appropriate indicators will be people's level of participation in this broader struggle for social change.

The author

Hilary Hughes de Rodríguez, Reproductive Health Adviser for GTZ, worked from 1987 to 1992 as the AIDS Programme Coordinator for AHRTAG, and was Editor of the international newsletter *AIDS Action*. She currently works in Zimbabwe.

An abbreviated version of this article appeared in 1992 in the magazine *AIDS in the World*. This version was first published in *Development in Practice* Volume 3, Number 1, in 1993.

Widows' and orphans' property disputes:
the impact of AIDS in Rakai District, Uganda

Chris Roys

IIntroduction

The problems of HIV/AIDS in Uganda, especially in the Rakai District, have been well documented.[1] A survey in Rakai in 1989 put the number of orphans at over 25,000.[2] The 1991 population census puts the number at 44,000.[3]

The Child Social Care Project (CSCP) in Rakai is addressing one of the social consequences of the AIDS pandemic: the property rights of widows and orphans — children under 18 years who have lost one or both parents. In partnership with the Department of Probation and Social Welfare in the Government of Uganda and Save the Children Fund (UK), the CSCP aims to develop the role of the Department in response to the enormous social problems arising from AIDS. Social workers and volunteers throughout the district are assisted to develop a community-based approach (as opposed to their traditional case-work role), and to coordinate services for vulnerable children.

Widows' and orphans' property disputes

Since April 1991, hundreds of disputes over property have been referred to the CSCP staff. Usually, a father and husband has died from AIDS, and other relatives have taken property from the widow(s) and orphans. In some cases, they have even evicted the woman and her children from the house, and chased them from the land.

The question of women's lack of right either to own or to inherit property has become a focal issue for women's empowerment and for development throughout Africa.[4] However, AIDS has brought mortality on an unprecedented scale, predominantly affecting those from 15 to 45 years, who tend to have dependent children. In some trading centres in Rakai, infection rates are said to be as high as 37 per cent.[5] Thus many widows are also infected with HIV. So, just at the time when they are least able to become economically independent, when they most need access to health care, a good diet and so on, they are denied it. Their children, who will probably be doubly orphaned, are likely to become homeless, landless, and uneducated, in a context where 90 per cent of the population depends upon subsistence agriculture.

There are three main interacting mechanisms which regulate inheritance in Rakai: wills, customary law, and statutory law.

Wills

These are a fairly modern idea, to which there is still considerable resistance. Firstly, illiteracy is high, especially among women, and written documents are an alien concept over which illiterate people have no control.

Many people are fearful of legal institutions and avoid contact with the law wherever possible. A written will is seen as a legal document and, therefore, to be avoided. Even more importantly, many fear that by making a will they will bring about their own death.

However, wills *are* written and do play a part in inheritance. A problem is that, in the face of illness, people with HIV infection sometimes assume that their death is imminent and make a will. Traditionally, the will is made in secret and given to one person to keep. However, patients often recover from the opportunistic infections associated with the disease, and can survive for many years before dying. Thus, they may make a will each time they think they may die. Thus there may be several wills held by different people, and conflict about which is the right one. In addition, a person's last verbal requests are supposed to be honoured, which introduces a further complicating factor.

Customary law

Under customary law and practice, issues of inheritance and the disposal of property (including widows and orphans, who are part of the estate) were decided by the family and clan members at the last funeral rites, which would take place up to a year after the burial.

An heir would be appointed, usually the eldest son, or the eldest male relative in the male line. In the case of a minor, the clan would appoint a caretaker until he reached an appropriate level of maturity to take on his responsibilities. The heir becomes the head of the family, and as well as being responsible for both the assets and liabilities of the deceased, he acts as the guardian of widows and orphans. In particular, the heir is given the residential house of the deceased and is not supposed to sell any land he has inherited, because (according to a Buganda saying) 'land belongs to a vast family, of which many are dead, few are living, and

countless members are unborn'. When a woman dies, her property (if any) may pass across the generational line, for example to a sister, but not to her children, as they belong to the male line.

In the past, the clan system was relatively strong and able to regulate inheritance satisfactorily. However, the processes of social, economic, and political change have reduced the importance of the clan — a decline that has been accentuated by the impact of AIDS.

Everyone in the community has been affected by the high rates of mortality, sickness, and bereavement. There is nobody who has not lost a close family member. For some, this has led to a sense of fatalism: 'We are all infected and are going to die'. While some have taken comfort in religion, others have adopted the attitude of 'grab what you can while you can'. Thus the authority of a clan which looks backwards and forwards over generations is undermined.

The people most directly affected by AIDS are young adults, including the more educated and wealthy, who would not otherwise have been expected to die. This too puts a strain on the clan system, as the people with greatest influence may already have died; and the eldest son and heir is often a young boy, rather than a mature man. The deceased may also have many dependants, whom other clan members will struggle to support. Customs of polygyny may complicate matters. When a man dies, he may leave several widows, each with orphaned children. In some cases, all the wives know each other and are aware of their relative status. In others, the fact that a man had several wives may emerge only at the burial. Thus, the relatives of different widows may compete to inherit property.

The sheer scale of the problem places a further burden on the families and the clan. Burials, once an unusual occurrence, are now an everyday event. Last funeral rites are now being combined with burials, in order to save time and money.

Statutory law

Where customary law fails, statutory law can be invoked.[6] This distributes property thus: 15 per cent to the widow(s), 75 per cent to the children, 9 per cent to parents and brothers, and one per cent to the heir. However, while the widow(s) and orphaned children have a right to stay in the house and land, this property still belongs to the heir. Nor is the widow the guardian of her children, responsibility for whom also falls to the heir.

The Child Social Care Project

The CSCP has developed a long-term, preventative approach to these problems, trying to change people's attitudes, beliefs, and behaviour. There are three elements:

● **Community sensitisation:** Conducting seminars with local officials in the district, notably chiefs (who are civil servants) and Resistance Councils (who are members of elected councils from village through to district), to inform them about the laws of succession, and about women's and children's rights.

● **Training:** Parish-level volunteers, known as child advocates, are trained in issues concerning children's rights and protection, including the property of widows and orphans. They can identify problems at an early stage and prevent them from getting out of hand. Other NGOs have also trained para-legals to assist in this process.

● **Writing wills:** CSCP staff, social workers, and volunteers encourage people to make wills, especially if they are already sick. This involves counselling to overcome the fears and resistance already mentioned, as well as help in writing the actual document. Local leaders are also involved in this process, to avoid the conflicts earlier described.

Many cases referred to the CSCP have required an immediate response, to prevent women and children losing their property, housing, and land. On referral, the social worker usually calls the complainant to the office to hear her side of the story, counsel her, and assess how to proceed. The next step would be to visit the site of the dispute and to seek audience with the other party. The social worker may be able to mediate at this stage. However, even if agreement is reached, it is important to involve other community members, so that the agreement is known, accepted, and upheld in the future.

The social worker's primary concern is to see that children are provided for adequately. Usually, this means acting as an advocate on behalf of the children and the mother. However, the social worker must also understand what will be acceptable to other members of the community, so that the widow and orphans will be supported and accepted by them.

Traditionally, the clan was important in settling inheritance claims, with its leader chosen for his wisdom and experience. However, this institution has been weakened, and it is now less effective and cohesive. The CSCP workers aim to strengthen the role of the clan. A meeting will be chaired by the clan leader, at which the social worker explains his/her role, talks about children's rights, and reminds the clan of its responsibilities. Both sides to the dispute are then heard, and opinions sought from members. The social worker helps the meeting to identify various options and come to an agreement, which is then forwarded to the Village Resistance Council.

The comprehensive Resistance Council (RC) system was introduced by the Ugandan government in 1986, incorporating all adults in the country through a series of interlinked committee structures. Where the clan is unable to resolve the dispute, or where its leaders have a personal interest in the case, the social workers involve the village RC. Again, the social worker will remind the Council about children's rights and inheritance law, and help the meeting to come to an agreed solution.

Recourse to statutory law may also be sought through the courts, if the clan or the village RC cannot resolve the dispute. However, even where magistrates make a ruling, the CSCP persuades them to attend village meetings to explain their judgements.

Case study

A social worker was called to attend to the case of a widow with three children aged 7 years, 3 years, and 7 months respectively. She wanted to return to her father's home, where she knew she would be assisted, together with her children and cattle. However, the heir refused to let her go. The Magistrate, clan members, relatives, and RCs in the area were invited to discuss to the case.

According to the clan leader, the husband had had seven wives and 20 children. Before he died, he had already allocated land to each of his wives. Other property was allocated to the children and widows by the clan after his death. This included cattle, some corrugated iron sheets, and barbed wire. It had also been decided that the deceased's motorcycle would be sold, and the proceeds distributed equally among the children.

However, this decision was later changed by some individuals without consulting the head of the clan. They allowed the heir to take the motorcycle, because he had not been allocated anything of his late father's property.

The 28-year old widow was the junior wife of the deceased. Since her husband died, she had encountered the following problems:

• She was no longer able to send her daughter to school, because she could not afford the fees.

• She had no-one to look after the cattle; she was responsible (as the junior wife) for attending to all the cattle before her husband died.

• She had to buy food, because her banana plantation was damaged by cattle belonging to the heir.

• The animals allocated to her and her children had no salt or drugs.

• The hut she lived in was on the verge of collapsing.

• She lacked essential domestic items, such as soap, salt, and paraffin.

She therefore decided to go to her parents, so that she could get assistance for her children. She had called the clan of her late husband to listen to her problems, but nothing positive had been done. She had often contacted the brothers and sisters of her late husband, but was referred to the heir, who was working far away from home.

So she called her relatives and asked them to decide what should be done next. Her father decided that, since she was not receiving any assistance either from the heir or from the clan, and her problems were not being addressed, he would obtain a permit to move the cattle belonging to his daughter and take her to his home.

When the 24-year-old heir heard of the move, he immediately took the matter to court, and the Magistrate made an injunction order stopping the movement of the animals until the matter was heard.

The widow also claimed that she had been given various items, including a room at a trading centre and some cattle for herself and her children, as well as the land already allocated to her by her late husband. Some of these had been taken by the heir.

The heir claimed that the widow had obtained a permit issued by the veterinary department to move the animals to her parents' home, without his knowledge, and that he should have been informed first. So he took the matter to court, and the movement of the animals was blocked. He stated that the widow was the cause of her own problems, since she had suggested that everyone should look after their own cattle.

He also complained that, unlike other children, he was not given anything during the distribution of property, yet he was also a son of the deceased.

Having heard from both sides, the CSCP team opened the meeting to other clan members, some of whose views are reflected below.

• The elder sister of the deceased said that the widow should go to her parents' home with all her property, including the children.

• A brother of the deceased said that the heir could take responsibility for supporting the widow, and then there would be no complaint. He said that the widow should go to her parents' home with the children, but leave the animals and any other property.

• Another sister of the deceased said that the meeting should decide, because she was at a loss to know what to do.

• The heir said that the widow could go with the child of 7 months, but should leave behind the other two children, together with their animals. The social workers asked him who should care for the children, but he was unable to answer, except to say that he had no home of his own and was not married.

• The Chairman of the RC suggested that an administrator of the deceased's estate should be appointed, with powers over everything, instead of investing powers in the heir, as was customary. He noted that some appointed heirs may be too young to manage family matters.

By now, the discussion had taken most of the day, without coming to a solution. The social worker suggested that time be given to enable both parties to study the whole matter again, with a decision to be taken in ten days' time.

On the agreed day the team went to the village, together with the Magistrate, to meet with the parents of the widow, the clan of the deceased, the heir, and other relatives, as well as neighbours and members of the general public. It was agreed that the widow,

together with her three children and the animals, could go to her parents' home, where she could be given assistance. Support would also be given by other paternal uncles who were present at both meetings. The children were free to visit their clan (their father's relatives), and this should be encouraged.

This case shows how complicated such issues are, with many people involved. It also indicates the amount of time that has to be devoted to the resolution of such conflicts. Two main issues should be emphasised.

Gender

The patriarchal nature of the society in which these conflicts take place is clearly the major issue. The clan system is patrilineal, and thus under customary law women cannot inherit property. This is because a widow may go back to her father's clan, taking any property with her, which would then be lost to the deceased's clan. This matter is related to the custom in some areas of widow inheritance.[7]

The woman has no entitlement to property — not even to her children, since they too belong to the clan, and the heir becomes their guardian. Male children will take up their position in the clan in due course, while girls will be 'sold off' for bride price.

Polygyny also discriminates against women and increases their vulnerability and that of their children, especially in relation to AIDS. In the case described, the deceased had seven wives. In some areas, child marriage is common, so a junior wife may be a teenager, while her husband is a man in his fifties. Modern statutory law also discriminates against women, specifying that 'a male shall be preferred to a female'.

The empowerment of women is the long-term solution to problems such as these, and in small ways the CSCP hopes to contribute to it. Clan and RC meetings tend to be dominated by men, and the social workers who facilitate them are very conscious of the need to ensure that women attend such meetings, and actively seek their opinions. However, although the female social workers provide a role model, it is hard to get women to express themselves freely in public. One possible solution is to hold some women-only meetings beforehand, although this can make the men suspicious and antagonistic.

Legal reform

Changes in the law are needed, to allow women to inherit on an equal basis with men. However, legal changes on their own will achieve nothing. The law in Uganda, for example, prohibits sexual intercourse with a girl under the age of 18 years, yet 'defilement' is common, and the law-enforcement agencies are reluctant to take any action.

The law has to be acceptable to people, otherwise they will disregard it. A process of education and sensitisation is needed to change attitudes. People must be involved in decision-making: thus, the law must be taken to the people, and not simply imposed from above.

Conclusion

The CSCP has had considerable success in settling individual disputes. More important, we have also had some success in enabling communities to deal appropriately with these conflicts without recourse to 'experts'.

Promoting the empowerment of women is important, but this phrase has become so overused that it is in danger of becoming meaningless. A vital aspect of empowerment is economic independence. In the CSCP we are involved in helping women to claim the right to own property, land, and housing, as well as to care for their children. While this will not in itself empower them, it will at least help women to achieve some degree of economic power to provide for themselves and for their children.

Notes

I am grateful to the project staff and especially Alex Bagarukayo, Gertrude Wanyana, and James Ssekinwanuuka for their contributions to this article. Any omissions and errors, however, are my responsibility.

1 A. Barnett and P. Blakie (1990): *Community Coping Mechanisms in the Face of Exceptional Demographic Change*, London: ODA; A. Dunn (1992): 'The Social Consequences of HIV/AIDS in Uganda', Overseas Department Working Paper No. 2, London: Save the Children Fund UK.

2 S. Hunter and A. Dunn (1991): *Enumeration and Needs Assessment of Orphans in Uganda*, London: Save the Children Fund UK.

3 *Population and Housing Census*, Government of Uganda, 1991.

4 D.M. Martin and F.O Hashi (1992): *Women in Development: The Legal Issues in Sub-Saharan Africa Today*, Washington: World Bank.

5 AIDS Control Programme, Rakai Report, Uganda, 1993.

6 Succession Act as amended by the Succession (Amendment) Decree 1972.

7 B. Olowo-Freers and T. Barton (1993): *Studies in Cultural Diversity*, New York/Geneva: UNICEF.

The author

Chris Roys has worked for Save the Children in the UK and in Uganda, where he is a social-work adviser in Rakai District. He is a qualified social worker and has a particular interest in child abuse and child protection, the impact of HIV/AIDS on children, and exploring methods of talking to and listening to children.

This article was first published in *Development in Practice*, Volume 5, Number 4, in 1995.

Annotated bibliography

Of the vast literature on health-related matters, we offer here a selective listing of recent and classic English-language publications that focus on the relationships between development and the politics of health. Some of the most penetrating contemporary work in this field has been undertaken by Southern feminist networks and women health professionals, in the context of women's health and rights, much of this in preparation for the 1994 International Conference on Population and Development. Their insights into exclusion, and the social institutions through which it is maintained, are of wider application in the field of health and development and hence are highlighted here. A sample of journals that take a multi-disciplinary approach to health matters is included, together with international health organisations and health-related networks.

Like the Reader itself, the bibliography is aimed at practitioners and academics with an interest in exploring the links between development and health. It does not cover detailed aspects of health care, nor does it include material of a highly specialised medical nature.

This Annotated Bibliography was compiled by Eleanor Hill, Deborah Eade, and Caroline Knowles (Editor and Reviews Editor respectively of Development in Practice), with assistance from Mohga Kamal Smith (Oxfam Health Policy Adviser).

Ehtisham Ahmad, Jean Drèze, John Hills, Amartya Sen (eds): *Social Security in Developing Countries*
Oxford: Oxford University Press, 1991
A broad-ranging collection of authoritative papers gathered under the auspices of the United Nations University, focusing on social security — including employment generation, provisioning of health care and education, land reform, food subsidies, and social insurance — and how State policies and public action can act to reduce human deprivation and eliminate vulnerability.

Marge Berer with Sunanda Ray: *Women and HIV/AIDS: An International Resource Book*
London: Pandora Press, 1993
An excellent overview of the issues relating to HIV/AIDS, covering all the necessary factual information regarding the disease and its transmission as well as descriptions of a wide variety of initiatives and projects to combat HIV. It highlights many issues which would otherwise remain hidden without its strong gender analysis.

British Medical Association: *Medicine Betrayed: The Participation of Doctors in Human Rights Abuses*
London: Zed Books, 1992
An authoritative and informative account of the responsibility of physicians to protect human rights, this provides a thoughtful ethical commentary, an overview of international law relating to torture and medical experimentation, and practical guidance for medical practitioners and policy-makers alike. The context in which doctors may commit gross violations of

human rights is itself one that is often conditioned by fear, ignorance, or extreme coercion. The Working Party which prepared this book addresses controversy and dilemmas head-on. Some recommendations are provocative and will stimulate productive debate.

Peter Coleridge: *Disability, Liberation, and Development*
Oxford: Oxfam (UK and Ireland), 1993
Taking as his point of departure the systematic oppression and marginalisation of disabled people, the author examines the social attitudes that give rise to such exclusion, and looks at ways in which it can be overcome. The book thus offers an insight into the processes of liberation and empowerment that are the touchstone of development.

Rebecca J. Cook: *Human Rights in Relation to Women's Health: The Promotion and Protection of Women's Health through International Human Rights Law*
Geneva: WHO, 1993
This document examines the relevance of international human rights to the promotion and protection of women's health, and provides a framework for future analysis and for collaboration among organisations concerned with these issues. The document explains the international, regional, and domestic mechanisms levels that are available for holding States accountable for their compliance with human-rights treaty obligations concerning women's health.

Sonia Correa with Rebecca Reichmann: *Population and Reproductive Rights: Feminist Perspectives from the South*
London: Zed Books in association with DAWN/New Delhi: Kali for Women, 1994
From a Southern feminist perspective, the authors consider conventional debates on population and examine the inter-linking of economic processes, demographic dynamics, and women's lives. Analysing the effects on women of past and present fertility-management policies, the authors argue for the indivisibility of health and rights. They identify the challenges to be tackled by women in the South, and suggest strategies for political action by the international women's movement.

Robert Desjarlais, Leon Eisenberg, Byron Godd, and Arthur Kleinman: *World Mental Health: Problems, Priorities, and Responses in Low-income Countries*
Oxford: Oxford University Press, 1995
Based on the collaborative work of over 120 experts worldwide, this book represents the first systematic attempt to survey the suffering caused by mental-health problems. It brings together information on mental illness and behaviour that influences health and potential for human development, and on the promotion of mental health as defined by the World Health Organisation — that mental health is not simply the absence of detectable disease, but a state of well-being in which the individual can fulfil his or her full potential. Arguing that there are diverse consequences of mental-health problems, and political, social and cultural forces which bear on them, the book provides examples, rather than bare statistics, to describe global patterns of problems and solutions. It shows how people in different settings deal with them and identifies opportunities for developing more appropriate interventions. It concludes with an Agenda for Action and an Agenda for Research.

Ruth Dixon-Mueller: *Population Policy and Women's Rights: Transforming Reproductive Choice*
Westport, Connecticut: Praeger, 1993
The author's thesis is that the exercise of women's reproductive rights depends fundamentally on the exercise of their rights in other spheres. Population-control policies and programmes would probably be unnecessary if women enjoyed their basic

economic, political, and social rights and had genuine reproductive choice. The author argues that by building on women's concerns about their survival and security, it is possible to address the coercive pro-natalism inherent in patriarchal inequalities in the family and society, without introducing an equally coercive `anti-natalist' agenda.

Deborah Eade and Suzanne Williams: *The Oxfam Handbook of Development and Relief*
Oxford: Oxfam (UK and Ireland), 1995
The first volume of this three-volume reference book introduces the approaches that inform Oxfam's work, focusing especially on human rights, social diversity, and strengthening local capacities. Chapter Five, 'Health and Development' is a comprehensive guide to topics such as the role of NGOs in health care, the policy framework, the health needs of specific population groups, health-care provision, and the financing, planning and evaluation of health programmes. Chapter Six, 'Emergencies and Development', also has full sections on health and nutrition, shelter, water and sanitation, vector control, and food security.

Hilary Goodman and Catriona Waddington: *Financing Health Care*
Oxford: Oxfam (UK and Ireland), 1993
In what has become a highly politicised ethical debate, this book goes beyond the ideological positions on public versus private systems of health care and examines the realistic options for poor communities to incorporate cost-recovery mechanisms for health and development services.

Andrew Green: *Introduction to Health Planning in Developing Countries*
Oxford: Oxford University Press, 1994
This book covers all aspects of planning for health in developing countries. Within the context of a PHC approach, it emphasises the many factors that impinge on health, the

different non-government agencies involved in health activities, and the need for participation in planning by communities. Equity is an important theme throughout the book. The need for combining planning techniques and political analysis is stressed, as is the importance of planning by a wide variety of professionals in addition to specialist health planners.

Trudy Harpham and Marcel Tanner (eds): *Urban Health in Developing Countries: Progress and Prospects*
London: Routledge, 1995
Specialists in public health and urban development offer an inter-disciplinary approach to urban health. They present recent research priorities and discuss the management and financing of urban health services; the role of international agencies such as WHO, the World Bank, UNICEF, and local NGOs; trends in urban health policy; and prospects for future improvements at strategic and conceptual levels.

Betsy Hartmann: *Reproductive Rights and Wrongs: The Global Politics of Population Control and Contraceptive Choice*
New York: Harper and Row, 1987 (revised 1993)
A critique of the economic, political, health, and human-rights consequences of population control as practised by the US population establishment, national governments, and international agencies. The author argues that the real solution lies not in coercive population-control programmes, but in the improvement of living standards, the position of women in society, and the quality of health and family-planning services. She calls for a fundamental shift in population policy towards the expansion rather than the restriction of individual reproductive choice.

Betsy Hartmann and James K. Boyce: *A Quiet Violence: View From a Bangladesh Village*
London: Zed Books, 1983

An inspiring insight into the reality of villagers' lives, this book shows the nature of the structural barriers faced in overcoming poverty and exclusion. The perspective and priorities of people who live on the margins of survival are distant from the world of governments and bureaucrats, which appears only in the form of local officials. The authors clearly show how much mainstream development fails to reach those most in need.

Lori Heise with Jacqueline Pitanguy and Adrienne Germain: *Violence Against Women: The Hidden Health Burden*
Discussion Paper No 255, Washington: The World Bank, 1994
This paper illustrates the extent and nature of the violence suffered by women around the world. It also describes some of the many initiatives underway to combat the problem, highlighting the ways in which health personnel in particular can be instrumental in this effort.

Najmi Kanji et al: *Drugs Policy in Developing Countries*
London: Zed Books, 1992
This book emerged from a review of the WHO Action Programme on Essential Drugs, and includes material drawn from 13 country studies. The authors find that the commoditisation of health in industrialised countries, and the transfer of this ideology to the developing world, has today created a context in which the rationalisation of drugs policies and efforts to control the activities of multi-national companies are widely seen as State interference in the free market. Analysing the political context, the authors define a framework within which to build rational drugs policies.

Korrie De Koning and Marion Martin: *Participatory Research in Health: Issues and Experience*
London: Zed Books, and Johannesburg: National Progressive PHC Network, 1996
Based on the presentations at a 1993 International Symposium on Participatory Research in Health, this book brings together a wide range of experience and perspectives. It covers issues such as training, planning, research methods, and evaluation from the angles of both academics and practitioner. Contributors are drawn from all parts of the world, and from many occupations. There are case-studies of participatory research as well as critical analysis of the processes which result in success and failure. The work raises critical issues such as gender, race, and class divisions, presenting these in the light of the different social, political, and economic contexts in which research has taken place.

Anne LaFond: *Sustaining Primary Health Care*
London: Earthscan (with SCF), 1995
The quality and availability of health-care services in developing countries suggest that support for them is not as effective as it might be. Programme benefits often fail to outlive external funding, and the aim to build sustainable services remains unmet. Reviewing experience in two African and three Asian countries, the author calls for an approach that addresses the wider structures and institutions that influence investment, planning, and management in the health sector.

John J. Macdonald: *Primary Health Care: Medicine in its Place*
London: Earthscan, 1992
The author presents a strong argument for the continued relevance of the PHC approach, as advocated at Alma Ata. The work includes a critical appraisal of the limitations of the medical model of health which still predominates among health professionals. It also argues for much better inter-sectoral collaboration in working towards health goals.

David R. Phillips and Yola Verhasselt: *Health and Development*
London: Routledge, 1994

Through a series of thematic chapters and regional and country case-studies, this book presents a broad but detailed description of the multi-faceted aspects of health and development worldwide. It focuses on issues such as the effects of economic adjustment and environmental change on health, the possibility of extending health services, socio-cultural factors in HIV/AIDS transmission, and the health of women beyond maternal and child health.

Jon Rohde, Meera Chatterjee, and David Morley: *Reaching Health For All*
New Delhi: Oxford University Press, 1993
This work reviews a range of experience in community health programmes aimed at achieving 'Health For All'. Descriptions of different projects reflect the many ways in which the principles and theories of PHC are put into practice. These are supplemented with critical analysis of why projects succeeded or failed. It is a valuable source of case-study examples and analysis for those struggling to implement PHC.

Gita Sen, Adrienne Germain, Lincoln C. Chen (eds): *Population Policies Reconsidered: Health, Empowerment, and Rights*
Boston, Mass.: Harvard Center for Population and Development Studies and International Women's Health Coalition, 1994
This book brings together writings by academics, policy-makers, health professionals, and activists in the fields of women's health and rights. From various perspectives and disciplines, the contributors argue that population policies should assure the rights and well-being of people who have already been born and who will inevitably be born, rather than attempting to limit the ultimate size of the world's population. Topics covered include sexual and reproductive health and rights, the women's health movement, population and the environment, human well-being and freedom, empowerment, and fertility control.

Patricia Smyke: *Women and Health*
London: Zed Books, 1991
This book examines the links between women, health, and development with the aim of providing a better understanding of women's health issues and the root causes of their problems. It offers a comprehensive overview of the major health issues facing women (serious illnesses, occupational health hazards, threats to mental health, reproductive problems, disability and ageing, and women as consumers of health-related products). Addressing the question of why women so often fail to get the health care and health information they need, the author discusses legislation, education, environmental factors, local customs and practices, armed conflict and violence. Initiatives to improve women's health status are presented, including health education, advocacy, use of the mass media, and networking. The book includes case studies, a resource guide, and suggestions for action.

Derek Summerfield: *The Impact of War and Atrocity on Civilian Populations: Basic Principles for NGO Interventions and a Critique of Psycho-social Trauma Projects*
London: ODI Relief and Rehabilitation Network Paper 14, 1996
New patterns of warfare mean that 90 per cent of victims of contemporary conflict are civilians. This paper is a critique of current methods of treating civilian trauma. It argues that it is not appropriate to take Western psycho-social models and impose them on other cultures. Psycho-social trauma projects must be more culturally sensitive; relief workers need to apply a thorough knowledge of the historical, social, and political impact of the conflict with which they are dealing.

Peter Townsend, Nick Davidson, and Margaret Whitehead: *Inequalities in Health: The Black Report and The Health Divide*
Harmondsworth: Penguin Books, 1992

Brings together two seminal works (the *Black Report*, first published in 1980, and *The Health Divide*, 1988) on the importance of poverty in determining health. Specifically examines the situation within the UK, looking at the differential health and illness patterns across class and income divisions. The two reports demonstrate conclusively the scientific evidence in favour of the need for action to reduce poverty and material deprivation in order to improve the standard of health in the population. As a result, the politics of health care is a strong theme throughout.

UNDP: *Human Development Report*
Oxford and New York: Oxford University Press (annual)
This annual publication, taking the view that development is necessarily people-centred, is a systematic attempt to identify and analyse those factors that can serve as indicators of human development (the Human Development Index). These include not only national economic performance, but also people's access to essential services, and the extent to which basic human rights are realised across a national society: how far people are, and feel, 'secure'. In 1995, the HDI was disaggregated, to produce the Gender-related Development Index (GDI). This reveals the nature and extent of women's exclusion both from the benefits of economic activity (such as improved health care and financial security), and from the opportunity to shape public policy. The *HDR* is, then, an excellent source of statistical information, and also demonstrates some of the ways in which social, economic, and political marginalisation affect people's lives.

Gill Walt: *Health Policy: An Introduction to Process and Power*
London: Zed Books/Witwatersrand University Press, 1994
An analysis of the many direct and indirect influences on policy-making in the context of health, this book offers a framework within which to go about influencing change. The author examines areas such as the role of special interest groups, how the policy agenda is determined, and the arenas within which government and international institutions operate. Given the speed at which reforms are taking place in the public sector, this book offers a valuable tool with which to understand, and to shape, the policy debate.

David Werner, Carol Thurman, and Jane Maxwell: *Where There Is No Doctor: A Village Health Care Handbook*
Palo Alto, CA: Hesperian Foundation, 1993 (revised)
One of the best-known and most widely translated books on community health care, this inspirational work (first published in 1977) explores the links between poor health and social, political, and economic exclusion. More than a self-help guide, it places empowerment, participation, and social justice firmly at the centre of development for health, arguing that 'the key to health lies in the people themselves'. It has been followed by several titles based on this philosophy, also published by Hesperian Foundation. Prominent examples include David Werner and Bill Bower (1982), *Helping Health Workers Learn*; Murray Dickson (1983), *Where There Is No Dentist*; David Werner (1987), *Disabled Village Children*; and Susan Klein (1995), *A Book For Midwives*.

World Bank: *World Development Report*
Oxford and New York: Oxford University Press (annual)
This annual publication reviews economic performance and trends and is a valuable source of information, as well as offering an insight into the thinking behind Bank lending policies. The *1993 WDR*, entitled *Investing in Health*, is of particular interest. It examines the interplay between human health, health policy, and economic development, and advocates a three-pronged approach to improving them.

Firstly, governments need to foster an economic environment that 'enables households to improve their own health'. Secondly, government spending on health should be re-directed to more cost-effective programmes that do more to help the poor. And thirdly, governments should promote greater diversity and competition in the financing of public health and the delivery of health services. Financing public health and 'essential clinical services would leave the coverage of remaining clinical services to private insurance, or to social insurance'. Further, the Bank argues, governments should encourage competition and private-sector involvement even in publicly financed health services.

WHO: *Primary Health Care — Report of the International Conference on Primary Health Care*
Alma-Ata, USSR, 6-12 September 1978, jointly sponsored by WHO and UNICEF, in *'Health for All' Series*, No. 1, Geneva: WHO, 1978
The original document describing the vision of Primary Health Care.

WHO: *Global Strategy for Health for All by the Year 2000*
in *'Health for All' Series*, No. 3, Geneva: WHO, 1981
This takes the PHC strategy further, with specific details of what must be done in order to achieve its goal of Health for All by the year 2000.

Journals

Contact
(published six times a year by the Christian Medical Commission of the World Council of Churches)
Written for the practitioner and general reader. Contains descriptions of a variety of health-related projects around the world, along with some more critical issue-based essays.

Health and Human Rights
(published quarterly by the François Bagnaud Center for Health and Human Rights, Harvard School of Public Health, ISSN: 1079-0969; Editor: Jonathan Mann)
An international journal dedicated to studying the relationships between human rights and health. The journal examines the effects of human-rights violations on health; the impacts of health policies on human rights; and the inextricable nature of the relationship between the promotion and protection of health and the promotion and protection of human rights.

Health Policy and Planning: A Journal on Health in Development
(published quarterly by OUP in association with the London School of Hygiene and Tropical Medicine, ISSN: 0268-1080)
Academic journal with a strong practical focus. Presents both research reports and critical essays on a wide range of health service issues. Includes a regular section of 'Ten best readings on ...', which is helpful in directing readers to a wider range of resources.

The Health Exchange
(published six times a year by the International Health Exchange, ISSN: 1356-3858; Editor: Isobel McConnan)
This bi-monthly magazine and its job supplement are published in the UK by IHE, which helps to provide appropriately trained health workers where needed in developing countries. The magazine explores issues, ideas, and practical approaches to health improvement in developing countries and

provides a forum for health workers and others to share viewpoints and experiences in this area. It is intended for all those with an interest in international health development, and combines features, information about jobs and courses.

Reproductive Health Matters
(published twice a year by *RHM*, c/o AHRTAG, ISSN: 0968-8080; Editor: Marge Berer)
An international journal dedicated to examining reproductive health matters from a women-centred perspective, and aiming to appeal to 'women's health advocates, researchers, policy-makers and health professionals at national and international level'. Each thematic issue contains a range of academic papers, local-level presentations, updates on current research, reviews and further resources. Subsidised rates are available for subscribers from developing countries.

Social Science and Medicine: An International Journal
(published bi-monthly by Elsevier Science Ltd, ISSN: 0277-9536; Editor-in-Chief: Dr Sally Macintyre)
An academic journal with both research and theoretical papers covering a wide range of health-related themes. It provides an international and inter-disciplinary forum for the dissemination of research findings, reviews and theory in all areas of common interest to social scientists and health practitioners and policy-makers.

World Health Forum: An international journal of health development
(published quarterly by WHO, ISSN: 0251-2432, available in Chinese, English, French, Russian, and Spanish editions)
A quarterly record of ideas, arguments, and experiences contributed by a wide spectrum of health professionals worldwide. Information ranges from critiques of conventional health policies, through lessons from project failures, to success stories illustrating the value of a new approach to technical solution. The goal is to communicate practical lessons that can bring the processes of health thinking and planning closer to real conditions in the field.

Organisations

The African Medical and Research Foundation
An independent NGO which works to improve the health of the people in eastern and southern Africa, AMREF runs a wide variety of innovative projects with an emphasis on appropriate low-cost health care. Its programmes include community-based PHC, training, AIDS and malaria prevention, family planning, and the famous Flying Doctor Service. AMREF publishes a wide range of health learning, research, and practical materials.

American Public Health Association
The APHA International Clearinghouse is a major centre for information on the health of women and children. It publishes a newsletter, *Mothers and Children* (in English, French, and Spanish), each issue of which focuses on a specific theme. The newsletter includes reports from practitioners as well as literature reviews on the chosen topic, and is available electronically through the *World Bank's PHNLink Network* and SateLife's *HealthNet* system. The Clearinghouse also has four information databases covering 15,000 primary documents; education materials; networking information on hundreds of relevant organisations worldwide; and periodicals.

Appropriate Health Resources and Action Group
AHRTAG aims to disseminate practical information on PHC and disability issues, and provide an information and enquiry service for community health workers. It runs a resource centre which contains over 19,000 books, journals, training manuals,

and reports focusing on the practical aspects of PHC and community-based rehabilitation, and compiles a bibliographic database (with *AHRTAG Update* available on subscription). AHRTAG publishes briefing papers, booklets, resource lists, and four international newsletters (*AIDS Action* ISSN 0953 0096; *CBR News* ISSN 0963-5556; *Child Health Dialogue* ISSN 0950 0235; and *Health Action* ISSN 0969 479X), which are all available free of charge to readers in the South.

Health, Empowerment, Rights, and Accountability

HERA is an international group of women's health activists working together to ensure implementation of the Programme of Action produced by the International Conference on Population and Development (ICPD) held in Cairo in 1994. Building on the Cairo Consensus, HERA advocates, designs, and implements strategies to guarantee sexual and reproductive health and rights, within the broader context of human rights and sustainable development.

The Inter-African Committee on Traditional Practices Affecting the Health of Women and Children

An NGO based in Ethiopia and active in 23 countries, which has campaigned vigorously against the practice of female genital mutilation (FGM), and has conducted research on other harmful practices relating to childbirth and delivery, social and nutritional taboos, the forced feeding of women, early childhood marriages, and teenage pregnancy.

International People's Health Council

IPHC is an informal network of groups and movements committed to working for the health and rights of disadvantaged people, and their liberation from poverty, hunger, and unfair socio-economic structures. Its members believe that health for all will be best achieved through participatory democracy, equity, and the accountability of governments and leaders to the people. IPHC facilitates information-sharing among its membership through a structure of regional representatives around the world.

International Federation and International Committee of the Red Cross

The ICRC is uniquely mandated to offer protection and assistance to victims of war and armed conflict, by means including the provision of medical aid. It has considerable experience in the field of war surgery and the psycho-social aspects of conflict. Publications are available in several languages, including English and French.

International Women's Health Coalition

IWHC is a non-profit organisation that works with individuals in Asia, Africa, and Latin America to promote women's reproductive health and rights. IWHC provides technical, moral, and financial support to reproductive health service-providers and advocacy groups in a number of countries, publishes books and position papers, convenes meetings on new or neglected issues in women's sexual and reproductive health, and acts directly to influence the work of population and health professionals, national governments, and international agencies.

Latin American and Caribbean Women's Health Network

Organises region-wide activities and publishes a quarterly magazine, *Women's Health Journal* (in Spanish: *Revista Mujer Salud*), which links about 2,000 groups and individuals worldwide, and is an international forum for researchers and women's health activists. The magazine addresses all aspects of women's health, and provides information about reproductive health and rights, pregnancy and childbirth, sexuality, HIV/AIDS, and occupational health.

Médecins Sans Frontières

MSF offers assistance to populations in distress, to victims of disasters, to victims of armed conflict, irrespective of race, religion, creed, or political affiliation. MSF is often the operational partner of UNHCR in refugee-related emergencies. MSF has published a series of specialised documents providing recommendations and information on procedures to assist doctors and paramedics working in isolated and often precarious conditions.

The Medical Foundation for the Care of Victims of Torture

A charity registered in the UK providing medical treatment, practical assistance, counselling and psychotherapy to survivors of torture. It also provides training for health professionals and publishes a range of reports, including the recent *Guidelines for the examination of survivors of torture.*

Save the Children Fund UK

SCF UK publishes research and working papers, and development manuals which are designed as short practical guides for development practitioners. Examples include *Toolkits: A practical guide to assessment, review and evaluation* (1995); *The Management of Health and Nutrition in Emergencies* (1996); *Children, Disability, and Development* (1994).

Teaching Aids at Low Cost

A UK NGO which distributes low-cost and appropriate books, slides, and teaching materials to developing countries by mail order. Topics in the TALC catalogue include Health Care Services; Mother and Child Health; Nutrition and Child Growth; AIDS Education and Communication; Education and Communication; Disability; Appropriate Technology. TALC has also developed small 'libraries' — collections of books aimed at pharmacies, district hospitals, district health workers, village and community workers, or medical students. Titles offered by TALC include: *Where there is No Doctor; Where there is No Dentist; A Book for Midwives;* UNICEF *State of the World's Children; Stepping Stones* from Strategies for Hope; *Women and HIV/AIDS.*

United Nations Children's Fund

UNICEF has a universal mandate to promote the survival, protection and development of children. It was the lead agency in developing the 1989 UN Convention on the Rights of the Child and the 1990 World Summit for Children. UNICEF collaborates closely with other UN agencies in programmes concerning health, nutrition, education, women and maternal health, and public and environmental health. UNICEF publishes widely, the most well-known of its annual publications being *State of the World's Children* and *The Progress of Nations*, both authoritative sources of information which give an overview of health-related issues from the perspective of children.

United Nations High Commissioner for Refugees

UNHCR is concerned with the international protection of refugees, defined as persons who owing to a well-founded fear of persecution for reasons of race, religion, nationality, social group, or political opinion are outside the country of their nationality; and the promotion of durable solutions for their problems. Publishes the annual *State of the World's Refugees* and various guidelines, for example on reproductive health (1996), sexual violence (1995), refugee children (1994), disabled refugees (1992), and refugee women (1991).

United Nations Population Fund

UNFPA is the lead UN agency on population issues, such as reproductive health, fertility, mortality, and demography; and on follow-up to the 1994 International Conference on Population and Development, held in Cairo. Its magazine *Populi* (available in English, French, and Spanish) is free of charge, and is a useful source of information from many parts of the world. Its annual publication *The State of World Population* is a summary and overview of the main issues and trends in the field.

The World Health Organisation

WHO's objective is 'the attainment by all citizens of the world ... of a level of health that will permit them to lead a socially and economically productive life'. Its Global Strategy to achieve 'Health for All by the Year 2000' is based on the primary health care approach (PHC). WHO has the leading role in international standard-setting in the field of health. It works mainly with governments to reinforce their health systems, and also promotes policy-related research on all aspects of health, as well as the needs of particular population groups.

WHO has a wide range of publications, from highly specialised books and journals to those for the general reader. It also produces newsletters, training, and advocacy materials (often free of charge and published in English, French, and Spanish) for health workers and non-specialists who deal with health-related issues. Examples are the briefing pack on Female Genital Mutilation (FGM), and The Mother-Baby Package produced by the Maternal Health and Safe Motherhood Programme. Its annual publications are *The World Health Report* and *World Health Statistics Annual.*

The WHO World Wide Web home page (http://www.who.ch) offers electronic access to information held at its Headquarters (such as statistics, publications, conferences), access to the six WHO regional offices, and to the WHO Library database (WHOLIS). Apart from WHO publications, this has extensive holdings of books, monographs, and other documents; and 3,000 periodical titles.

Addresses of publishers and other organisations

African Medical and Research Foundation, PO Box 30125, Nairobi, Kenya. Fax: +254 (0)2 506112.

Allison and Busby, 5 The Lodge, Richmond Way, London W12 8LW, UK.

American Public Health Association (APHA) International Clearinghouse, 1015 Fifteenth Street NW, Washington DC 20005, USA. Fax: +1 (0)202 789 5600.

Appropriate Health Resources and Action Group (AHRTAG), 29-50 Faringdon Road, London EC1M 3JB, UK. Fax: +44 (0)171 371 7104.

Earthscan Publications, 120 Pentonville Road, London N1 9JN, UK. Fax: +44 (0)171 278 1142.

Elsevier Science, The Boulevard, Langford Lane, Kidlington, Oxford OX5 1GB, UK.

Harper and Row, 10 East 53rd Street, New York, NY 10022, USA.

Harvard School of Public Health, 8 Story Street, 5th Floor, Cambridge MA 02138, USA. Fax: +1 (0)617 496 4380.

Health, Empowerment, Rights and Accountability (HERA), c/o International Women's Health Coalition, 24 East 21st Street, 5th Floor, New York, NY 10010, USA. Fax: +1 (0)212 979 9009.

The Hesperian Foundation, 2796 Middlefield Road, Palo Alto, CA 94306, USA. Fax: +1 (0)415 325 9044.

Inter-African Committee on Elimination of Harmful Practices, PO Box 3001, Addis Ababa, Ethiopia.

International Committee of the Red Cross, 19 avenue de la Paix, 1202 Geneva, Switzerland. Fax: +41 (0)22 734 7979.

International Federation of Red Cross and Red Crescent Societies, PO Box 372, 1211 Geneva 19, Switzerland. Fax: +41 (0)22 833 0395.

International Health Exchange, 8-10 Dryden Street, London WC2E 9NA, UK. Fax: +(44) 0171 379 1239.

International People's Health Council (IPHC) Information can be obtained from the Hesperian Foundation, or from CISAS, Apartado Postal 3267, Managua, Nicaragua. Fax: +505 (0)2 24098.

International Women's Health Coalition, 777 UN Plaza, New York, NY 10017, USA. Fax: +1 (0)212 687 8633.

Kali for Women, B1/8 Hauz Khas, New Delhi 110 016, India. Fax: +91 (0)11 686 4497.

Latin American and Caribbean Women's Health Network, RSMLAC, Casilla 50610, Santiago 1, Chile. Fax: +56 (0)2 634 7101.

Macmillan Press, Houndmills, Basingstoke, Hampshire RG21 2XS, UK. Fax: +44 (0)1256 842084.

Médecins Sans Frontières, 8 rue Saint-Sabin, 75544 Paris Cedex 11, France. Fax: +33 (0)1 48 066868.

Medical Foundation for the Care of Victims of Torture, 96-98 Grafton Road, London NW5 3EJ, UK. Fax: +44 (0)171 813 0011.

The Overseas Development Institute (ODI), Portland House, Stag Place, London SW1E 5DP, UK. Fax: +44 (0)171 393 1699.

Oxfam (UK and Ireland), 274 Banbury Road, Oxford OX2 7DZ, UK. Fax: +44 (0)1865 313925.

Oxford University Press, Walton Street, Oxford OX2 6DP, UK. Fax: +44 (0)1865 556646.

Pandora Press, c/o Harper Collins, 77-85 Fulham Palace Road, London W6 8JB, UK.

Fax: +44 (0)181 307 4440.

Penguin Books, Bath Road, Harmondsworth, Middlesex UB7 0DA, UK. Fax: +44 (0)181 899 4099.

Praeger Publishers, 88 Post Road, Westport CT 06881, USA.

Routledge, 11 New Fetter Lane, London, EC4P 4EE, UK. Fax: +44(0)171 842 2303.

Save the Children Fund UK, Mary Datchelor House, 17 Grove Lane, London SE5 8RD, UK. Fax: +44 (0)171 222 7500.

Teaching Aids at Low Cost (TALC), PO Box 49, St Albans, Herts AL1 4LX, UK. Fax: +44 (0)1727 53869.

UN Development Programme (UNDP), One United Nations Plaza, New York, NY 10017, USA. Fax: +1 (0)212 826 2058.

United Nations Population Fund (UNFPA), 220 E 42nd Street, New York, NY 10017, USA. Fax: +1 (0)212 557 6416.

United Nations High Commissioner for Refugees (UNHCR), Centre William Rapard, 154 rue de Lausanne, 1202 Geneva, Switzerland. Fax: +41 (0)22 739 8111.

United Nations Children's Fund (UNICEF), UNICEF House, 3 United Nations Plaza, New York, NY 10017, USA. Fax: +1 (0)212 888 7465.

The World Bank, 1818 H Street N.W., Washington DC 20433, USA. Fax: +1 (0)202 473 1782.

The World Council of Churches, 150 Route de Ferney, PO Box 2100, 1211 Geneva 2, Switzerland. Fax: +41 (0)22 791 0361.

The World Health Organisation (WHO), 20 avenue Appia, 1211 Geneva 27, Switzerland. Fax: +41 (0)22 791 0746.

Zed Books, 7 Cynthia Street, London N1 9JF, UK. Fax: +44 (0)171 833 3960.